More Praise for *Engage Your Brand*

"The Archer Group has ushered us into this brave new world with great insight and a keen focus on our customers and our brand. Looking forward to our continued participation in this evolving social conversation!"

Lisa Wollan, Head of Consumer Insights & Brand Strategy, Wawa, Inc.

Thanks Lisa! We owe you a bottle of Malbec!

By now every marketer knows the Web has quickly become a primary marketing channel. But how to get your brand into the mix? Lee and Patrick have the answers. They'll show you how to join the social marketing party using skills you already possess and they punctuate the ideas with case examples that prove the points. So what do you have to lose? I'll tell you what you might lose—if you don't jump in, you'll lose market share to those who already know the stuff in *Engage Your Brand*."

David Meerman Scott, bestselling author of *The New Rules of Marketing & PR* now published in 24 languages

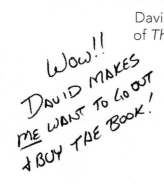

Wow!! David makes me want to go out + buy the book!

↳ David is much more social than we are — we'll be there some day!

"Over a decade ago, Lee was the "tech guy" who convinced me that South Park games built with Flash would make ComedyCentral.com more popular than the sites for NBC or Fox. Lee built those games and he was right! Years later I realized that Lee's unique talent isn't his engineering skill — it is his ability to explain how and why new web applications are so important to our brands and our customers."

Larry Lieberman, President, Forever Wild Productions, Formerly VP Strategic Planning and New Business Development, Comedy Central

MY FIRST MEETING W/ LARRY INVOLVED ME DOING AN ELEVATOR PITCH FOR SOUTH PARK GAME IDEAS. TALK ABOUT PRESSURE!!

"*Engage Your Brand* is filled with insightful, practical and short case studies and very clearly shows marketers how to effectively use social media to engage with customers. The book is a quick read filled with useful tips on how to be authentic, interactive and immediate. This is a must-read for CMOs pondering how to better embrace social media."

Chuck Martin, Best-selling author, CEO, Net Future Institute, #1 professor on Twitter

GREAT!! GUY.. TOLD US TONS ABOUT PUBLISHING A BOOK!

And who would you trust more?! Thanks Chuck!!

We are drowning in information but starved for knowledge.

John Naisbitt

ENGAGE YOUR BRAND

HOW SMART COMPANIES ARE USING SOCIAL MARKETING TO DRIVE THEIR BUSINESSES FORWARD

LEE MIKLES AND PATRICK CALLAHAN

THE
Archer
GROUP

ENGAGE YOUR BRAND

HOW SMART COMPANIES ARE USING SOCIAL MARKETING
TO DRIVE THEIR BUSINESSES FORWARD

Lee Mikles and Patrick Callahan

233 N. King Street
Wilmington, Delaware 19801
t 302/429.9120
f 302/429.8720

Continue the conversation at www.EngageBlog.com.
Learn more about The Archer Group by visiting www.archer-group.com.
To report errors, please send a note to eyb@archer-group.com.

NOTICE OF RIGHTS

NOTICE OF LIABILITY

TRADEMARKS

First Edition: March 2010
Layout by Amanda Jones

Printed in the United States of America

ISBN 978-0-557-37799-2

10 9 8 7 6 5 4

To our families, both at home and at work, who helped us put our thoughts on paper and drove us to create something very special.

To Tom, who saw a book in us, even when we didn't.

And to the members of The Archer Group—who motivate us every day to bend the rules on behalf of our work and our clients.

WHO SHOULD READ THIS BOOK?   17

You're a smart marketer. You understand the major influence the web is having on the business world, and you know you can't afford to miss a major shift in the way marketing is done. This is not a tutorial for Facebook or Twitter. It's a guide for marketers who want to know how to use social media correctly, to avoid the ramifications of using social marketing poorly.

WELCOME TO THE PARTY   23

Social marketing is causing a major shift in how brands interact with consumers, but its concepts shouldn't be completely foreign to marketers. Sure, the technology that makes social marketing work is new, but the concepts behind it are as old as human interaction itself. It's not about what you've learned by being a marketer; it's what you've learned by interacting with other people.

If you've been to a dinner party, you already know a lot about social marketing; the same rules and etiquette apply. Offer consumers something of value, listen to their opinions, tailor your conversations, and don't just talk about yourself.

SAY GOODBYE TO THE ONE-WAY CONVERSATION   37

We are moving from a "marketing to" approach to an "interacting with" approach. Marketing is no longer a one-way conversation, and consumers expect brands to engage them, not merely broadcast advertising messages. And whether or not you choose to engage your brand, these conversations are occurring; people are out there talking about you. Are you going to join in and help steer the conversation?

VALUE: IT'S NOT ALL ABOUT THE BENJAMINS 55

While traditional advertising is designed primarily to explain a product's value, social advertising itself must have value. You shouldn't think of value just in terms of dollars and cents. Think of value as being like the value you'd get out of a good conversation. You are marketing to individuals with emotions and desires, not shoppers. So go ahead, give your customers what they want.

THE SOCIAL MEDIA MARKETING TRIANGLE 75

Brands must find opportunities to create the social media triangle, where conversations are occurring among the brand and the consumer as well as between consumers. These three-way conversations can create a social marketing bonfire, which has the potential to last much longer than a traditional marketing campaign. Remember, social marketing has a different lifecycle than traditional marketing, without a predestined end date.

AUTHENTICITY REQUIRED: FAKERS BEWARE 93

There is now a public forum, unlike any other, for people to share their experiences, so your brand is accountable for all of its actions. That's why brands must be authentic, owning up to their mistakes and letting people in on how things really are. Authentic conversations will be rewarded by loyalty. Any attempt at being anything less than genuine and authentic about your brand, product, or service will fail.

GET THAT MOTIVATION IN LINE 105

Brands must understand what motivates people if they want to influence what they do as consumers. Take some time to study psychologist David McClelland's "Theory of Learned Needs", which says people are motivated by a desire for achievement, affiliation, and power. True, this theory is the work of a 1950s psychologist, but it has a place in the social marketing world.

We've expanded McClelland's "Theory of Learned Needs" to include what motivates people in the social world: the chance to be the comedian, the philanthropist, the expert, or the maven, and to be recognized.

NOBODY PUTS SOCIAL IN THE CORNER

It's time to empower your employees to interact with the public. Nuke your Twitter department, because social can't be confined to a tiny corner of your organization. Weave social marketing throughout everything you do, and you'll really maximize its power. And don't just leave it up to the interns. You want to put your best players in the game, and give them the tools they need to succeed. Don't weigh them down with stringent corporate rules, but rather give them loose guidelines that'll give them the leeway to interact creatively, all the while acting in a way that's consistent with your brand image.

ASSEMBLING YOUR A-TEAM

Begin your social media efforts with a clear plan that involves the right people and starts with listening. By assembling your A-Team, you are defining the role the rest of your organization is going to play, and getting the right people on board to make things happen. Here's whom you'll need: the digital genius, the content creators, the listener, and key people from other departments. Once you get your team together, study what other relevant brands have done in the social world before making your grand entrance.

RETHINKING ROI

Rather than concentrating on how certain metrics from traditional marketing don't work with social, you should instead rethink ROI from the ground up when deciding how much to invest in a social marketing campaign. Take into consideration the qualitative and quantitative benefits and the impact to other areas of the organization.

WHAT'S NEXT

The pace of change in social networking shows no sign of slowing down. Platforms will wane in popularity, and new ones will emerge to take their place. Consumer willingness to share will continue to be at odds with a desire for privacy. All of these changes will happen swiftly and without fanfare. Marketers need to stay focused on the fundamentals of starting a conversation and learn along the way.

PREFACE

About the Photos

Since Flickr is arguably the largest social photo site, with users sharing over 4 billion photos on the site, we thought that it would be a perfect exercise to see what photos could be crowd sourced for the book. We posted a few keywords for each chapter and asked people to submit photos that they thought "fit the bill." What you see in the book are the photos we selected, along with the photographer's Flickr username or website in case you want to see the rest of his or her work. There is no shortage of talented photographers on Flickr, and we are grateful that they allowed us to use their handiwork!

About the Rest of the Book

This book started as a passion project between Patrick and Lee—hoping to put words behind their frequent presentations and client discussions. As the project evolved, more people from the company got involved: from the book's layout, infographics, and copy editing, to the book's website (www.EngageBlog.com), it truly became an Archer project. With each team member's contribution, Patrick and Lee knew that the bar was rising on their contributions, simply to keep up with the magic being created around them.

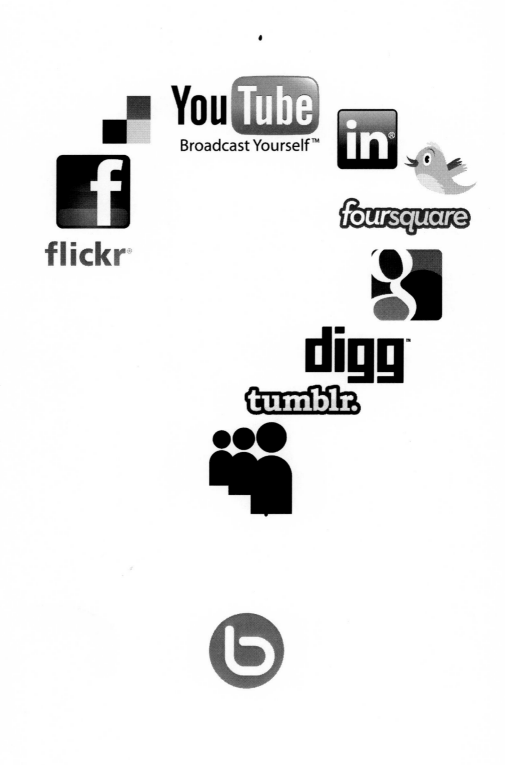

Introduction

WHO SHOULD READ THIS BOOK?

You're a smart marketer. You understand the major influence the web is having on the business world, and you know you can't afford to miss a major shift in the way marketing is done. This is not a tutorial for Facebook or Twitter. It's a guide for marketers who want to know how to use social media correctly, to avoid the ramifications of using social marketing poorly.

Maybe you're already sold on the idea of social marketing, but you just need more information to persuade your team to adopt it. This book will give you the information to allow you to do that, so you can help your company adapt to the marketing changes that are well under way. You can truly *engage your brand.*

BEGIN WITH THE END IN MIND

In Stephen Covey's now-classic *The 7 Habits of Highly Effective People*, one of the first key habits discussed is to "begin with the end in mind." It's helpful to understand and envision what your marketing may look like *after* social media has been integrated successfully into your marketing mix. Consider the following four cornerstones to guide and build your vision:

MARKETING WILL BE AUTHENTIC

Knowing that your consumers will hold you accountable, your marketing will focus on delivering value, rather than simply catchy tag lines and fancy product shots.

CONSUMERS WILL HELP YOU MARKET

You needn't lose sleep over the thought of having to interact with a million consumers at the same time. Consumers will help you spread your message, deal with detractors, and point your brand in the right direction.

MARKETING WILL OCCUR EVERYDAY, BASED ON A CONTINUOUS STREAM OF CONVERSTIONS

Your marketing message will be a living, breathing dialogue, incorporating real-time feedback to influence what happens next. You'll have specific information on how your brand message is working in time for you to react to the feedback.

YOU'LL SEE YOUR BRAND THROUGH YOUR CUSTOMER'S EYES

Since you as the marketer will have the connection to the consumer, complete with specific conversations as reference points, you'll be the one in the company who can paint the whole picture of how your consumer sees your brand, and what everyone needs to do to get it right.

The face of marketing *has* changed—and you have to as well. You're reading this book because you realize that you have a new vision you need to understand and communicate so that your company fully embraces this new way of thinking. While reading this book, keep in mind these four cornerstones of how you'll operate at the end of the day.

AN EVER-CHANGING FUTURE

At the time that this book was written, Facebook, Twitter, and YouTube were household social brands, while MySpace was fading and foursquare was rising. Had this been written 18 months earlier, the social media landscape would have been totally different. Only time will tell which sites or apps people will be raving about from one day to the next.

Regardless of the platforms du jour, the concepts outlined in *Engage Your Brand* remain unchanged. Consumers want honest interactions from brands, and the brands that can meet those needs will build strong bonds with consumers. If you can engage your brand around the current social media landscape, you'll be well positioned to adapt to new platforms as they emerge.

ARE YOU READY?

chapter one

WELCOME TO THE PARTY

When Ron Alsop was writing *The Trophy Kids Grow Up: How the Millennial Generation Is Shaking Up the Workplace*, he noted the difficulty he was having reaching his interviewees via email. Replies were sporadic at best, making it difficult for him to complete his book. Ron then tried connecting to these Millennials (those born between 1980 and 2001) via Facebook. The responses were almost instantaneous!

Less than ten hours after a magnitude 7.3 earthquake devastated Haiti in January 2010, CNN reporter Anderson Cooper jumped into a plane and flew to get a firsthand look at the damage and rescue efforts. From the cab ride to the airport to the UN chopper flight over Haiti, Anderson used Twitter to update his 400,000 followers with a raw feed of the news.

These examples highlight the major shift that has begun with social media—and the social media "Big Bang" is still occurring. Facebook reports having over 350 million users, more than the population of the United States. These people are active, with over half of them accessing it daily, posting over 3.5 billion status updates, links, and photos or sharing whatever else might be on their mind, at any time.

In his book *Bowling Alone: The Collapse and Revival of American Community*, Robert Putnam asserts that our society needs and wants "social capital." If we agree, then social media is that social capital. Facebook, Twitter, YouTube, and countless other social media networks are connecting people. These sites are the new virtual bowling alleys where we meet and interact.

Social marketing is causing a major shift in how brands interact with consumers. But this shouldn't be completely foreign to marketers. Sure, the technology that makes social marketing work is new, but the concepts behind it are as old as human interaction itself.

DON'T BE "THAT GUY"

We've all seen him. He's *that guy*, the pompous man at the dinner party who spends the evening bragging about himself and his accomplishments, rather than engaging others in conversation. By the end of the night, he's alienated almost everyone at the party, and has left the other guests wondering, "Who invited that guy, anyway?"

Social marketing isn't what you've learned as a marketer; it's what you've learned by being a good guest at a dinner party. The same etiquette and rules apply to social marketing:

BRING A BOTTLE OF WINE

Presenting the hosts with a nice bottle of wine tells them you appreciate having been invited to the party. When establishing your brand's presence, offer consumers something of value—deals, special privileges, insights—to show just how much you appreciate being welcomed into the conversation and that you care about them.

LISTEN

In *Never Eat Alone*, Keith Ferrazzi writes that "[y]ou should be governed by the idea that one should seek first to understand, then to be understood." In other words, listen before you speak so you know what to say. Social marketing is about listening. While this may sound counterintuitive for any marketer who grew up on terms like "reach and frequency" and "share of voice," you need to listen closely to understand what exactly your customers value.

TAILOR YOUR CONVERSATIONS

A gifted conversationalist will tailor the conversation to the interests of each particular person he or she encounters. If you just repeat the same story over and over at a party, not only will you get a reputation for being a bore, but your story isn't likely to connect with your fellow partygoers. Marketing is no longer a "one-size-fits-all" conversation. Successful social marketing involves interactions that are tuned clearly to the individuals on the other end of the conversation.

DON'T JUST TALK ABOUT YOURSELF

Just talking about yourself will turn other people off, and you'll end up having people avoiding you by the end of the night. Likewise, brands are learning that talking about themselves exclusively doesn't cut it in the social marketing world. You need to find out how to create a dialogue about what the user values, which is, likely, not always your brand.

SHOW UP ON TIME

If a distant relative throws a party, you might get away with showing up late or skipping it entirely. But missing your best friend's engagement party? Not a chance. With social marketing, the bigger your brand, the more noticeable your absence from the party will be. A recent Cone study found that 93% of social media users believe a company should have a social media presence.

The Social Marketing Party is under way, and you don't want to miss it!

WHY THE PARTY ANALOGY WORKS

If **social networking** is the party, the place where people come together and interact, then **social marketing** is the conversation that takes place at that party. Consumers are starting to see brands as being more like people and expect them to act accordingly. If a brand isn't willing to engage them, they'll tune it out—just like they would do with that annoying guy at the party. Consumers are already at the party, and brands just need to find a way to get an invitation.

WHY YOUR BUSINESS NEEDS SOCIAL MARKETING

- Consumers are **overwhelmed with traditional marketing practices**, seeing an average of 3,000 marketing messages a day. They are paying less and less attention to these advertisements and becoming more distrustful of them.

- Your business can **build lasting relationships** with consumers and earn their trust by maintaining a dialogue with them.

- You can **learn what consumers are thinking about**, and use this to enhance your marketing practices.

ALL I NEEDED TO KNOW ABOUT SOCIAL MARKETING I LEARNED FROM DALE CARNEGIE

Remember that Dale Carnegie book *How to Win Friends and Influence People*? Originally published in 1936, the self-help behemoth has sold over 15 million copies and continues to influence how people view personal and business interactions.

Erik Qualman, author of the book *Socialnomics*, wrote

"[s]ocial companies in social media act more like Dale Carnegie and less like [advertising guru] David Ogilvy."

DALE CARNEGIE'S

Six Ways to Make People Like You

1 Become genuinely interested in other people.

2 Smile.

3 Remember that a person's name is to his or her ears the sweetest and most important sound in any language.

4 Be a good listener. Encourage others to talk about themselves.

5 Talk in the terms of the other person's interest.

6 Make the other person feel important and do it sincerely.

All that's listed here is fairly common sense, right? It's all stuff we learn by simply being human. Successful social marketing asks your brand to come down from that marketing Mount Olympus to start interacting with consumers on a personal level.

While traditional marketing practices have all but ignored Carnegie's list, social marketers are utilizing it, some with more success than others. Consider the case of two banks, ING Direct and Wachovia.

Case Study: ING Direct vs. Wachovia

In one corner, we have Wachovia, that faithfully fields customer service questions Monday through Friday using their Twitter account. In the other corner, we have ING Direct, that uses Twitter not only to handle customer complaints but, more importantly for marketers, also to create a dialogue about saving.

@Wachovia

Wachovia appears to have two employees supporting their online social media. It signs on at 8 AM and say something like, "Hi, this is Dave. I'm here

> Hi, this is Dave. I'm here and ready to accept your customer service request.

and ready to accept your customer service request." At 5 PM, Dave signs off, and thanks everyone for being loyal customers.

Most of the customers use Wachovia's Twitter as a customer service line, flooding Wahovia with very visible complaints, and the bank hasn't provided any motivation for people to stay engaged except for complaining. Wachovia has entered the social marketing party with a shiny new complaint box.

@INGDirect

ING Direct takes a different approach. It's Twitter not only fields customer service questions, but also provides a stream of suggestions and articles about saving money. For example, at the start of the fall sports season, ING Direct posted a link to a *USA Today* article titled "10 ways to save money on your child's sport." While these tweets might not have anything to do with ING Direct, they do make a connection between "the bank" and "saving money" in the minds of consumers. The tweets also motivate those who are interested in saving money—and who isn't?—to interact with socially savvy ING Direct.

Remember the dinner party scenario that we discussed earlier? **Tailoring your conversation** is key to being "a hit" there, and it's this ability that makes ING Direct's Twitter effort such a success. By monitoring keywords in people's

(continued)

(continued)

posts, ING Direct **listens** to what people are saying and responds accordingly. When someone posts, "I'm saving for college," ING Direct responds, "It's great that you're saving for college. Here are some other ways you can do it." Whether that person is an ING Direct customer or not, he or she will likely come away with a positive view of ING Direct, because ING Direct is **adding value** to the conversation.

> It's great that you're saving for college. Here are some other ways you can do it.

THE VERDICT

Imagine that both of these companies are guests at a party. Wachovia walks up to a group of people and announces, "It is 9:00 PM, and I am ready to partake in this conversation." This sounds pretty unnatural, doesn't it? Then ING Direct walks over to the group and, after listening to the chatter, joins the conversation with an interesting anecdote. ING Direct ends up being a big hit at the party, while the other guests are left wondering, "Who invited Wachovia?"

> It is 9:00 PM, and I am ready to partake in this conversation.

ING Direct is **interested in what others have to say**— not only about the company, but also about people's financial and life goals. Wachovia, on the other hand, instead of inviting people to engage it in a **genuine dialogue**, is only open to criticism.

chapter two

SAY GOODBYE TO THE ONE-WAY CONVERSATION

Imagine you're a record company about to release the definitive Mozart boxed set. Traditionally, you'd take out ads targeting the people you thought most likely to enjoy classical music—older, wealthy, educated people. But, Lee's 13-year-old daughter has a ton of classical music on her iPod and $150 of babysitting money. While traditional marketing overlooks her, social media lets you reach her. You can put all the marketing dollars you want into *New Yorker* magazine ads, but without social media marketing, you're still going to miss this consumer.

Engaging your brand using social media isn't just about marketing more efficiently to the *segments* you traditionally appeal to; it's about establishing conversations with individuals that you wouldn't have been able to find otherwise. These newly mediated conversations focus on interests, rather than demographics; on everyday topics, rather than household incomes. As consumers continue to reject mass marketing via DMAs, brands need to recognize that people are increasingly in control of the marketing conversation. By finding and listening to such otherwise-overlooked conversations, you're shifting your business practice from marketing to a mass of faceless consumer segments to **having *meaningful, engaging* conversations with real people**.

In the past, conversations were controlled by those with the loudest voices. Newspaper editors wrote editorials, politicians gave speeches, and advertisers broadcasted their messages to shape brand perception. **This was the one-way conversation** approach, where only those with resources had a voice. Maybe everyone else could get their opinion out there with the occasional letter to the editor, but there weren't many places where the average person could sound off to be heard.

Today, marketing is evolving from a highly scripted broadcast to a real-time exchange of value, which is driven by consumers. With iPhone in hand, the average person is standing up and proclaiming, "This is what I think!" Now everyone has the potential to shape public opinion or at least add their own to the mix. These **conversations are happening**, and they're only getting louder. It's up to you if you're going to join in and have your say.

Forget Demographics—Start Marketing to People.

BIGGER ISN'T ALWAYS BETTER

In the past, bigger brands could win the marketing battle by virtue of their size. They had more money to spend, and they spent it by scooping up the biggest and best advertising slots. But with social marketing, it's not necessarily the bigger brand that will win; **the better one will win**. Just ask Zappos, whose bear hug

on customer service and social marketing took it from an idea to a $1.2 billion Amazon buyout in just ten short years of selling shoes.

FORGET "MARKETING TO"—"INTERACTING WITH" IS THE NEW BLACK

We are moving from a "marketing to" (or clubbing consumers over the head senselessly in 30-second intervals) approach, to a conversational, "interacting with" approach. In the old days, you might win over consumers based on the strength of your marketing message. But this is no longer the case. Traditional marketing isn't going away—no advertising outlet has disappeared, from AM radio to TV. However, consumers are now wanting and expecting to participate in the conversation.

BE AUTHENTIC OR PREPARE TO BE EXPOSED AS A FRAUD

Just as you would rather talk to the authentic person at a cocktail party (rather than "that guy"), consumers would rather interact with a brand that truly engages them in a genuine way. Honest answers can generate tons of loyalty. And consumers, who are usually on the lookout for sales pitches, can recognize "the real thing." So they're far more likely to trust a brand that isn't trying to sell them something at every turn. Show consumers that you want them to get just as much out of the interaction as you do, and that authenticity will smooth over many rough patches.

YOU DON'T NEED TO OUTRUN THE BEAR

No, you don't need to have the number-one social media marketing campaign in the world. If you're into mountain biking and harpsichord playing (hopefully not at the same time!), there will probably be different conversations around those interests, with various people involved.Having a successful social marketing strategy is kind of like outrunning a bear while on a camping trip: you don't need to be the world's fastest runner, you only need to be faster than the other campers. Likewise, you don't need to be the best social media marketing guru on the planet, just better than the other marketers out there when it comes to striking up the same conversation.

Case Study: Brands Win by Admitting They Don't Have All the Answers

And guess what? That's OK. Check out these brands that have found success by **admitting they don't have all the answers**.

WET SEAL is a clothing store for teenage girls that has a member-driven feature on their website called "The Runway." It allows customers to "create outfits." By selecting items from the e-store, they create a personalized closet and create customized outfits, which can be viewed by other member-shoppers, who can then mix and match from this closet until they find the combination they like best. They can even vote for the top outfits, which are featured by clicking the "See Top Rated Runway Outfits" link. With this customized outfits function, Wet Seal is essentially inviting its young consumers to contribute to this conversation called fashion. The company is saying, "Yes, we know that we've got great products. But we aren't the final authority on what's in style—you are! We want to see what you think works." This acknowledgment has certainly paid off. Customers who partake in Wet Seal's create-an-outfit feature have ended up **spending 20% more at checkout than those who don't use it.**

DELL's IdeaStorm website gives users the opportunity to sound off on everything from which features they'd like to see on future laptops, to the troubleshooting issues they're encountering with current computers. More than a mere

(continued)

(continued)

comment box, IdeaStorm allows Dell to **have a dialogue**
with consumers, and keeps people up-to-date on what
changes they're implementing based on the consumer
suggestions. IdeaStorm even has a real affect on future
production; **with each release cycle, Dell has produced
laptops based on IdeaStorm feedback**.

THE VERDICT

Both Dell and Wet Seal are **engaging their customers** and
are being rewarded financially as a result of this marketing
approach. Both companies have a solid foundation of
quality products to build upon, and both have a lot riding
on being able to accurately predict consumers' needs. Dell
and Wet Seal have found ways to engage consumers and
get them invested in the success of their favorite brands.

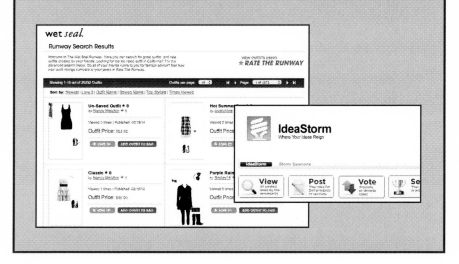

SOCIAL MEDIA IS IMMEDIATE—AND SO IS CUSTOMER FEEDBACK, FOR THAT MATTER

Thanks to social media, your company will be held **instantly accountable** for any beef an unsatisfied customer might have with you, before you even have a chance to respond. In his book *Socialnomics*, Erik Qualman reports that 80% of tweeting is done from mobile devices, so consumers can literally broadcast their experience **during the experience**. Talk about immediate feedback!

In the good old days, an angry customer might vow never to buy from you again, and then go home and vent to a few of his or her friends. Sure, that was bad enough, but what about now? A customer gets upset, and **one angry tweet later, hundreds or even thousands of people know about it**. On the flip side, social media has made it possible, and highly acceptable, to report positive experiences as well.

LEE'S MOBILE PIZZA

One summer night, Lee was running late (as usual) to get home from work. Having dinner responsibilities, he did what most tech-dads would do in that situation: he fired up his iPhone and ordered a pizza from Domino's. The entire process was accomplished at a stoplight.

FEEDBACK TIMELINE

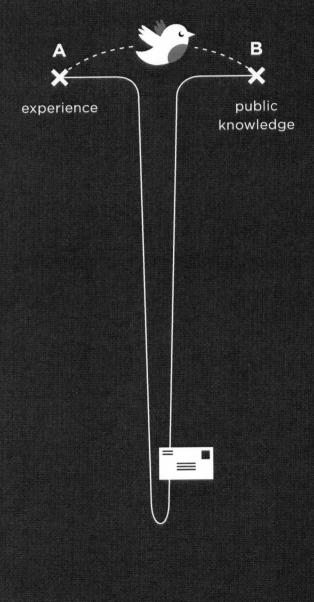

A   B

experience   public knowledge

Lee was so impressed that he tweeted about the experience:

> *Just ordered pizza using Domino's mobile site while @ stoplight. This is how mobile should work!*

Less than an hour later, Domino's picked up his comment and tweeted back to thank him for sharing his experience. This honest exchange showed Lee that it listened. Domino's did something right, and all hungry souls listening to either one of them at that moment now knew that the Domino's mobile ordering platform is worth a try.

THOSE FANTASTIC FANS: BRANDS LOVE THEM, AND CONSUMERS DEPEND ON THEM

A fan is someone with a passion for your product. While a mere **consumer** might buy your product without feeling a special bond with the brand, a fan will express his or her interest by posting about you on Facebook, or engaging you in conversation by way of Twitter. It's important to build a social media marketing strategy that gives fans a chance to interact and spread the word about your company.

Here are a few things you should consider:

- While the term might evoke images of screaming girls meeting the Beatles at the airport, **fans** are really about having **relationships**, not about unquestioning adoration. Brands shouldn't take their fans for granted.

- People are depending more and more on **social news**—news that they get from other consumers, rather than from marketing departments or news outlets—to make informed purchasing decisions. Authentic public accolades from fans do influence future buyers.

- Some fans desire **discretion** and won't be as vocal as others. For instance, adults who use Depend undergarments wouldn't want to stand up and shout, "I wear adult diapers, and I hate them!" But they *would* value a private social network where they could perhaps discuss concerns with other Depend users.

- Common sense will tell you if discretion is something your fans want and need.

Case Study: Social Media Gets the Bills Paid

THE PROBLEM

A firm that we are close to helped a company—we'll call it Lighthouse—create a website. The relationship was a strong one for years and the firm helped Lighthouse transition to self-managing the site. After delivering on everything expected of the firm, they sent Lighthouse a final bill. But, Lighthouse didn't pay. The firm went through the normal routes, asking for payment and resending invoices four or five times, as per their request. Still, the money wasn't coming in.

As often happens in client relationships, people from the firm had become friends with a few of the people at Lighthouse in real life as well as on Facebook. Informally, Lighthouse confirmed the quality work the firm had accomplished and assured them that everything was complete, but privately said that times were tight for Lighthouse.

Then, during a conference on entrepreneurialism, the CEO of Lighthouse stood up. He bragged about how strong the company was, how it was a model for budding businesses to follow, how it was committed to helping entrepreneurs in the region. We were there with friends from the firm getting stonewalled, and they showed a collective face of shock and anger.

(continued)

(continued)

We understand that sometimes businesses have cash flow problems. It happens. But, it's one thing for them to tell our friends, "Hey, we're a little short on cash right now, but we'll do what we can to make payments." It's quite another for them to publicly boast about how great they're doing, while privately avoiding their business partners.

THE SOLUTION

Finally, emotions got the better of the principals of the firm. One of them posted a Facebook status update saying, "I wonder when Lighthouse is ever going pay their bills?" A few hours later, they started receiving frantic phone calls from people at Lighthouse. They were about to go into a meeting with potential investors with their new business model— social media marketing. They knew if their investors started doing some digging on the tubes and wires of the Interwebs, they'd likely find what was written about their deliquencies.

After some discussion, a face-to-face visit (and a final resending of the invoices), the checks started rolling in. Every month, the firm is getting a little bit of money, and they are finally knocking down the total bill.

IMPLICATIONS

Social media provided a transparency to Lighthouse's business dealings that didn't put them in the "best light". When Lighthouse's lofty marketing efforts were coupled with the reality of their accounting efforts, the picture wasn't very pretty.

Conversely, the principals at the firm recognized that they had a heavy responsibility in their social actions. If they had been wrong in their accusations, or there were problems with their deliverables, they would have been the ones left with egg on their collective face. This illustrates that social media marketing is not just about marketing; it really affects every way your company relates to the public—including accounts payable and customer service. Because, if anything goes wrong, a consumer can express their unhappiness with you publicly, online. Social media marketing is more than just marketing. Social media marketing is about conversations with consumers.

SOCIAL IS HERE TO STAY—SO YOU MIGHT AS WELL GET USED TO IT

Back in the mid-'90s, companies wondered if investing in websites would be worth the cost. Not only would developing them require new budgets, but, at that time, they were still largely untested. Fast-forward 15 years, and websites have become pretty much indispensable for any business. Can you imagine a major player *not* having a website? Just like websites, social media is evolving, and that's why jumping into the social media marketing game now will provide you with the crucial experience you'll need down the road. Here are other reasons why you can't afford to wait:

- **Consumers expect to have a way to interact with your brand**. If you don't give them an outlet, they'll start seeing your brand as being out of touch, just like a company that has no website.

- **You need to experiment now** to discover what works for your brand. Get in there and learn what's of interest to consumers—*and what they want to talk about*—before your competitors do. Imagine that you're a hiking equipment manufacturer and one of your competitors has already engaged consumers in a conversation about the outdoors. You'll have a lot of trouble attracting people to your own conversation after the fact, because your competitor has already created one and is talking with them.

EXPERIMENT NOW!

chapter three

VALUE: IT'S NOT ALL ABOUT THE BENJAMINS

Kogi Korean BBQ may have the best tacos in LA, if not the world. But don't expect to enjoy them sitting down unless you bring your own table and chair. Kogi operates four taco trucks that move around the city to serve its loyal crowd. While traveling taco trucks may seem like a bit of a reach in terms of an analogy for social media marketing, Kogi provides some excellent lessons. The company uses Twitter adeptly to deliver value to thousands of potential customers, all without giving away a single Kimchi Melt.

Kogi tweets the locations of its lunch trucks—along with its drivers' names—every day, letting loyalists know where they can scoop up some of Kogi's tasty tacos. Additional tweets highlight unique items, short-supply items, or even the locations of LA's infamous traffic delays. With over 50,000 followers on Twitter, these tweets keep Kogi clearly in mind for fans to schedule their lunch plans. Kogi delivers value through social media marketing.

When you think about what value means to a consumer, you might assume coupons or special savings are what he or she craves. But really, **value may have nothing to do with money**. Try to think of value in terms of a good conversation. Good conversations tend to be informative, entertaining, and interactive. The value of a conversation is quantifiable only by you. And the same is true with social marketing interactions. **Value is *user-defined*.**

While traditional marketing drives you to continue broadcasting self-serving messages, social media marketing says **your messages must be of value** to people, or these customers will just tune you out. It's no longer about the value of your offerings that you market; it's about what value your marketing offers.

Case Study: Give 'Em What They Want

While traditional marketing explains a product's value, social media marketing must reflect value in and of itself. That's exactly what Sharpie and Toys"R"Us are doing, giving consumers the value they need to keep them engaged.

SHARPIE understands that **brands can no longer dictate their own value; consumers do**. It has set up "Sharpie Uncapped," a section of their website for users to post the different ways they're using the brand name's fine-point markers. Sharpie invites individual users to "[u]ncap what's inside." Some people decorate sunglasses or create Christmas ornaments—it doesn't really matter to Sharpie. The company has simply given customers an outlet to define what value the Sharpie brand holds for them, to share their love of the brand, and to build relationships with others who also love Sharpie.

TOYS"R"US rewarded loyal customers by making their Black Friday deals available only to the fans of their Facebook page. By doing so, Toys"R"Us not only showed their appreciation for their fans; it has also **provided reasons for new people to converse with them**. Imagine how valued these fans would feel if Toys"R"Us used them to help select the next Black Friday deals!

THE VERDICT

People want more than just a marketing pitch by way of social media, and that's where Sharpie and Toys"R"Us succeed. Instead of broadcasting messages about how great they are, these brands are giving people the information *they* need to utilize their products better. They **nurture fan interaction by offering value in their marketing through social networking**.

CIRCLE OF VALUE

Five Criteria to Value

1. MAKE YOUR AUDIENCE FEEL SPECIAL

We all love it when the bartender at our favorite haunt knows our name. It cements our connection with the place and makes us more likely to come back with friends to show off our VIP status. The Pit, a great barbecue place in Raleigh, North Carolina, uses the social networking application foursquare to get to know its VIPs. Foursquare uses a smartphone's GPS to let people "check in to" the location and share that information with others. The most frequent "checker" for a location is named its "mayor," an honor displayed to all others who check-in. Yes, it's a small title, but it's one coveted by many. The race for mayorship leads to frequent check ins and increased business for places listed on foursquare. The Pit expands that value by regularly giving the mayor and his or her friends free lunch or drinks. By creating a VIP status, the Pit offers a value that can't be conveyed with a 30-second radio spot or an impersonal coupon.

2. UNDERSTAND YOUR AUDIENCE'S *CIRCLE OF VALUE*

When a golfer buys a golf glove, he or she isn't just interested in golf gloves; we can be 99% certain that he or she (or for whomever the glove is being purchased) is interested in golfing. It seems pretty straight forward, but this point is something that many marketers miss with social media marketing. For the golf glove purchaser, his or her circle of value isn't a conversation about golf gloves alone, but playing better golf. So you shouldn't be restricted to talking only about your products. Instead, understand what else the consumer is interested in when using your products. Find a common point within that circle of value, one that surrounds your product and your consumer.

3. PROVIDE SOMETHING CONSISTENT WITH YOUR BRAND IMAGE

Are you giving away free t-shirts just because you've got a bunch lying around the office? That's OK. But, giving consumers something that further connects the consumer to your brand—now that's value to both the consumer and your brand.

Redwood Creek Winery's "Blaze the Trail" section of its website gives people the chance to earn "virtual corks" by uploading pictures to be shared with others on the site. The corks can be traded in for original prints or other Redwood Creek memorabilia, such as bottle openers. Every step of the way, from the digital corks to the real-life memorabilia, Redwood Creek does a fantastic job of keeping the prizes consistent with its brand image. Fans value the reward beyond its cash value, because the reward is earned through a genuine dialogue with the brand.

TRANSFER VALUE

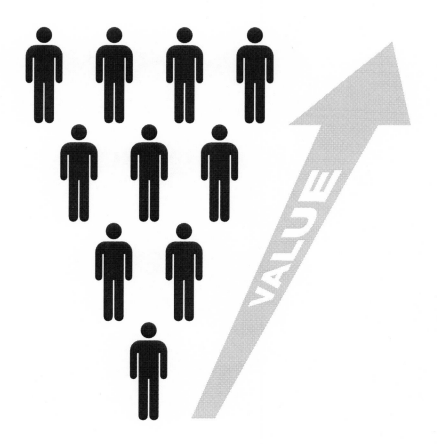

4. PROVIDE SOMETHING WITH *TRANSFER VALUE*

Something with transfer value is seen as valuable enough that the recipient wants to pass it along to others. We've all been emailed funny JibJab animated cards or videos of kids falling off skateboards. You might have enjoyed the humor, but you'll only pass these things along if you think they'll be of value to others. If an item has transfer value, it has the potential to go a lot further than a traditional ad or coupon. Social media marketing can extend its reach well beyond your initial distribution list.

For those who don't live in the Northeast, there's an amazing chain called Wawa, which has over 500 stores—each of which is like a convenience store on steroids. Wawa offers great custom sandwiches and have an extremely loyal following. In support of Wawa's 2009 cold beverage campaign, we created the "Dress-Your-Bottle" microsite to raise awareness of Wawa's store-branded juices and teas. The site let people dress up the beverage of their choice in a variety of costumes—ranging from a tough hockey player to a hot movie star—and then to share it with their friends.

All of this was designed with transfer value in mind, and the microsite provided a solid arena for customers to start conversations about Wawa. And, if the comic value wasn't motivation enough, Wawa offered a prize to the person whose dressed-up bottle received the most votes for creativity. This gave consumers a reason to encourage others to visit the microsite and have them support their best-dressed bottle or to dress up their own bottle for competition. Over 10,000 dressed-up bottles were created, attracting over 50,000 visitors to view and vote on their favorite bottle during the six-week campaign.

5. CREATE REASONS TO RETURN

Once you establish a solid relationship with consumers, you want to keep them coming back for more. Create something that will evolve, and people will be more likely to come back to repeat and refine their experiences. Redwood Creek Winery's "Blaze the Trail" website section continually adds new art and photographs. As mentioned previously, regulars receive digital corks for interacting on the site, which can then be redeemed for prints of Redwood Creek art and photographs. This creates a great incentive for people to continue earning these digital bits of value and makes frequent visits a must for wine enthusiasts.

Case Study: Wawa Hoagiefest 2009

In 2009, we helped Wawa tap into something people value— the **chance to be famous**. The campaign wasn't about giveaways. It was about allowing Wawa fans the chance to get creative and express their enthusiasm for the brand.

THE WEBSITE

Wawa's summer hoagie promotion, Hoagiefest, had a "summer of love" music festival feel in the stores and in traditional advertising. As part of the campaign, we added a video contest to help celebrate the tastiness of hoagies by channeling the good times of Woodstock. We asked Parry Gripp, lead singer of the pop band Nerf Herder, to create '60s-inspired—and hoagie-themed!—songs. Then, we gave Wawa fans the opportunity to create and upload music videos for these songs. Wawa encouraged everyone to share their videos with friends, and to vote for their favorite ones—all for a chance to earn a little fame and win a free hoagie party.

THE FAN REACTION

Wawa received a lot of creative and truly hilarious videos, and fans were rewarded by having thousands of people

(continued)

(continued)

see them in silly wigs lip-synching to groovy songs about sandwiches. Some videos got as many as 20,000 views, and we had over 500,000 people visit the *Hoagiefest* site— which, by the way, is about how many people attended Woodstock four decades ago. Far out! It looks like rock isn't dead after all.

WHY IT MATTERS

Since consumers control the conversation, your organization must contribute value through social media marketing to make them stay engaged. Remember, you're marketing to individuals with their own emotions and desires, not just the faceless shopper from a particular demographic. So you truly have to understand what real people care about. With this campaign, we helped Wawa build relationships with its faithful following, along with a host of invitees who visited the microsite, and not simply by giving away free sandwiches. Wawa tapped into what customers value: **fame, connectedness to the brand, and a chance to be viewed by friends as someone special**.

SOCIAL MEDIA MARKETING ISN'T JUST FOR THE ÜBER-FAN

You might think social media marketing caters too heavily to the sometimes relatively few super-loyalists, those 5% of über-fans who'll spend hours interacting with their favorite brands online—much of which might be wasted on the other 95% of customers. Malcolm Gladwell describes these über-fans, or trendsetters, as "Mavens" in his book *The Tipping Point*. These mavens derive great value in being seen as "in the know" by others. Jeep® tapped into this with its Jeep Experiences site, where people can post proof of their off-road adventures by clicking on the site's "Captured: Photos by the People" link. Most Jeep® owners might not ever take their vehicle to the Grand Canyon, but they can enjoy looking at pictures of someone else's trip there. By checking out what the über-fans are doing, "the people" can share that same passion and connection to a brand as much as the fiercest of fanatics.

Case Study: Where Traditional and Social Marketing Meet

The effort of **where you place your energy in marketing is changing**. You now need to spend more time getting people to interact with your brand, and less time singing its praises. Single-malt-scotch distiller Balvenie understands this and recently ran an ad in *The Wall Street Journal* to promote its online community, Warehouse 24.

THE AD

The ad features a picture of its scotch alongside the words: *"I enjoy spending a quiet evening at home discussing the finer points of a complex single malt with a few thousand friends."* The copy doesn't merely tout the quality of its product. It promotes **category awareness** by mentioning single-malt scotch, and, more importantly, it encourages people to check out Balvenie's online community, Warehouse 24.

THE ONLINE EXPERIENCE

Warehouse 24 provides tools—such as a tasting journal—that help broaden a customer's experience with a range of scotches, while connecting scotch enthusiasts all over the

(continued)

(continued)

world. The social tasting journal provides reference points to describe unfamiliar scotches, making it a valuable tool for the scotch drinker who wishes to expand his or her horizons.

WHY IT MATTERS

The ad isn't about the taste or other product features. Balvenie's understated ad shows a company directing its energy to drive people in a different direction—to an online community rather than a shopping center. If traditional marketing can show you images of an exclusive nightclub or a classy lifestyle, social media marketing invites you to step past the velvet rope and join the fun.

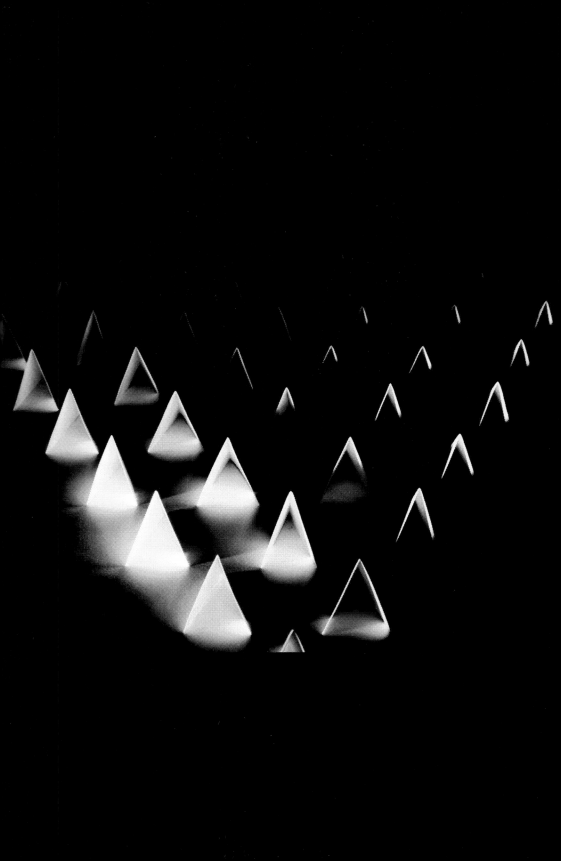

chapter four

THE SOCIAL MEDIA MARKETING TRIANGLE

As part of our social media listening, we noticed Wawa fans were using the phrase **"Wawa run"** to describe a visit to their local Wawa. Co-workers would announce "need coffee; gonna do a Wawa run" via Twitter. College students would tell their friends about study avoidance with a cute "ugh—need a break; Wawa run to the rescue!" The brand listened to its consumers, and the "Wawa run" was heard.

Flickr Photo by Wes Peck

Armed with this new lingo, we created the Wawa Run
Facebook application, where consumers could easily
notify co-workers, friends, dorm mates, and so on of
a pending Wawa run via Facebook. This app also let
fans send each other virtual coffees, hoagies, and other
Wawa products with a short message. Wawa listened to
its consumers and used social media marketing to keep
the conversation going. Each day, hundreds of Wawa
runs and virtual hoagies are sent between consumers.

While traditional marketing is typically one-way, from
the brand to the consumer, social media marketing
involves conversations **between** brands and consumers.
But these conversations can be very time-intensive
for brands and difficult to maintain in the longer term.
The real social media marketing power occurs with
networking, when consumers talk to each other about
brands. This consumer-to-consumer brand conversation
is the critical leg of a sustainable social media marketing
triangle.

The social media marketing triangle is a natural flow
of conversations, with the brand acting as a participant
rather than the sole speaker. This triangle can only
happen if you, as the brand, can create a reason for
these people to participate in the triangle, talking both
about and *with* your brand.

Conversations surrounding your products are already
occurring between consumers. So your goal as a brand
marketer is to offer enough value for consumers to want
to include your brand in these ongoing conversations.

Traditional marketing completed one leg of the triangle, from the brand to the consumers. Another leg of the triangle, conversations between consumers (a.k.a. word of mouth), has always existed; technology simply made it easier to share. Social media marketing connects these conversations—by forming an engaged network—to complete the triangle for the brand.

A strong social media marketing triangle is enormously powerful for the brand, where consumers drive the conversations, with the brand adding input to "stoke the fire." As Don Draper said in the great advertising television drama *Mad Men*, "If you don't like what's being said, change the conversation." While you can't always follow Draper's advice, engaging your brand in the social marketing triangle provides you with a great opportunity to nudge the conversation along in the direction most advantageous for your brand.

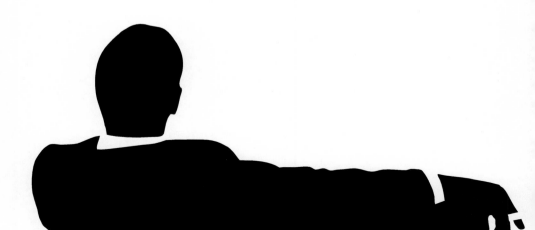

THE OLD WAY

TRADITIONAL MARKETING

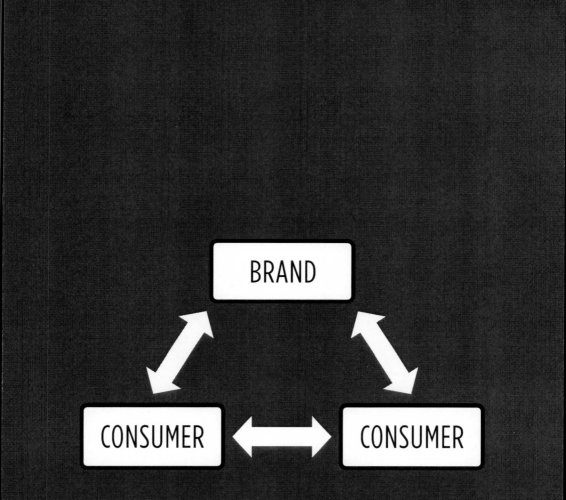

NIKE CONVERSATIONS GO THE DISTANCE

Lee had never been a runner, and that started all the way back in high school. Back then, you never wanted to be the last kid to finish your assigned laps during gym class. Because if you finished last, you had to run an extra lap. Lee was always the one running that extra lap. It took more than 20 years for Lee to change his mind about running.

Today, Lee is a running fanatic, thanks to the efforts of Nike and Apple. Back in 2006, the two companies combined to create the Nike+ device, which paired Nike's running shoes with the Apple iPod. You could now listen to your iPod while you ran, all the while tracking your workout, counting your calories burned, and monitoring your pace. After you returned from a run, you could sync your iPod to your computer. Your results would be stored online and you could then share them with millions of other Nike+ users.

Nike and Apple have created the world's biggest running club, and a very interactive one at that. Nike and Apple have created a social media marketing triangle around running and have created legions of fanatical users.

As expected, the website for Nike+ is all about running. You can see visualizations of your run, and slice and dice your data until your heart's content. Running is very much a personal sport, where you set goals for yourself. Nike+ offers all sorts of goal-building advice and incentives.

But Nike took this conversation one 'step' further, by making it easy for its consumers to interact with others on the site. You can challenge others to hit certain goals, such as miles logged or fastest 5K. Every run updates the comparative chart, showing progress and even allowing you to "trash talk" your opponents. This dialogue among runners brings people back to the site, further strengthening the triangle.

Runners have logged over 190 million miles on the Nike+ website. The tens of thousands of challenges between runners on the site shows that the social media triangle works. Nike provided the tools and the motivation to spark the running flame, and consumers turned it into a bonfire with their challenges, trash talks, and continued involvement. Every interaction is an active conversation with and about Nike (mediated by Apple).

Nike went even one step further by organizing the NikePlus Human Race, a global 10K race to be run simultaneously around the globe using NikePlus.com. In 25 cities, from Tokyo to Istanbul, runners gathered together in person. Runners didn't have to be in the cities to participate; they simply needed to log their 10K run on race day. In the buildup to the 2009 Human Race, over 140,000 runners participated in NikePlus training runs, logging miles and communicating with each other and the Nike brand.

So how do you build a social media marketing triangle when you aren't the Swoosh™? Just check out W.L. Gore's "Warm and Fuzzy" triangle.

Case Study: The Warm and Fuzzy Triangle

W.L. Gore has built a business on keeping people warm and dry with their GORE-TEX® membrane. And it has found a way to use the social media marketing triangle to start conversations with consumers.

The GORE-TEX® fabric is found in premium outerwear, and it keeps you warm and dry in the harshest of weather conditions. The gloves, jackets, and boots are a standard for any outdoor enthusiast. The company introduced a WINDSTOPPER® product line targeted at women, and it wanted to create an innovative campaign to connect with these consumers. This campaign became known as the "Give a Warm Fuzzy, Get a Warm Fuzzy" campaign.

The "Warm and Fuzzy" campaign targeted female consumers who had a passion for the outdoors. It provided these women with a chance to raise money for their passion projects by connecting with each other and Gore's WINDSTOPPER® brand. GiveAWarmFuzzy.com enabled visitors to vote for their favorite charity and enlist the support of others to join the discussion and/or donate to these special causes.

The site made it easy to invite others into the conversation and also personalized this interaction *visually*. The site displayed a participant's reach, creating a "family tree" of sorts, where she could see how the people she had

(continued)

(continued)

invited were furthering the cause by inviting others. This visual display of a person's reach got women talking, inviting others if only to see their own tree grow across the country. By **establishing a dialogue** with consumers, and then **giving them the tools** to converse with each other, we established a social media triangle that required only Gore's passive participation to sustain the conversation.

In three short months, over 1.5 million votes were cast on GiveAWarmFuzzy.com, creating a social media marketing triangle that Gore can continue with women long after the campaign.

WANTED: HIGH-QUALITY COMMENTATORS; NO REFERENCES NECESSARY

Media mogul Rupert Murdoch recently acknowledged that traditional media sources are becoming less influential, falling victim to social media's growing influence. These days, you don't have to be a *New York Times* columnist to have a voice, because the average person now has a forum to unleash his or her opinions onto the world. It's no longer the reputation of the publication that matters so much; **it's the quality of the message that makes people perk up** and pay attention. When was the last time you bought something on Amazon.com *without* reading the reviews posted by previous consumers? TripAdvisor.com is a site dedicated to reviews from regular Joes, not famed "reviewers." These comments on Amazon and TripAdvisor are filtered further as people ask others, "Was this review helpful?" Conversations are occurring, and quality conversations are being promoted to be heard by many.

It's time for brands to listen to what's important to their customers. Forget focus groups. Focus instead on the stream of information consumers broadcast every day via social media.

It's the quality of the message...

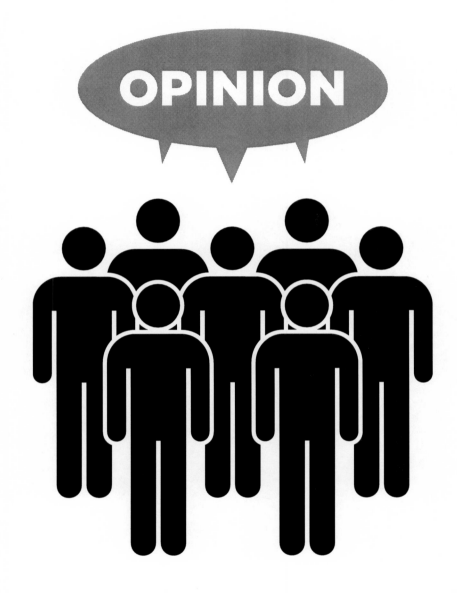

...that makes people perk up.

Listen to What's Working.

Are customers raving about a new product that you just introduced? Did they go crazy for that funny video you posted? These social media cues provide great feedback for you while you're just starting to engage in this process. Find out what's working and what's not while you still have a chance to fix and fine-tune the conversation.

Listen to Their Interests.

Because you need to be marketing to people, not to consumers, you shouldn't only take an interest in what they're saying about your brand. People who buy your candlesticks to stage homes might only talk about candlesticks once a month. But they talk about what it takes to sell homes every day, all day. Get your brand into those conversations and you'll see that there will be plenty to talk about.

Listen to the Complaints.

Maybe there's a lot of buzz online about how your customer service stinks or that your new product is a dud. Don't be too discouraged. Instead, think of it in more productive terms. Getting **negative feedback can be a moment for your brand to shine**. Solve a person's problem on Twitter and the world gets to witness your customer focus firsthand.

DON'T FIZZLE OUT—BE THE BONFIRE

John Willshire, head of innovation at London's PHD Media, made a great analogy for how we look at marketing. **Traditional marketing is like a firecracker**. It goes off with a bang and a brilliant flash, but it fizzles out quickly. **Social media marketing is like a bonfire**. It takes a while to build, but it endures and can continue to grow. The relationships you build with social media marketing may take time to establish, but, once in place, you can use them to ensure your continued presence in the consumer conversation. Like a bonfire, social media marketing has a different lifecycle than traditional marketing, with no set end date once it has been initiated. **The big challenge today** is knowing how to utilize traditional marketing firecrackers to spark interest and then create a social media marketing bonfire, which will keep the flames of interest both high and hot.

First and foremost, when thinking of using social media marketing, you should remember **that this is not just your conversation; it belongs to your customers**. So you should act accordingly. Use the manners your mother taught you, as if you were entering a conversation at a party. If you broadcast your message without conversing, you'll be like a firework or that annoying party guest. You might make a loud noise, but people will hold their ears until you're done talking. Keep things warm and inviting, like a bonfire.

chapter five

AUTHENTICITY REQUIRED: FAKERS BEWARE

In *The Catcher in the Rye*, Holden Caulfield is always accusing people of being phony. He often uses the word "phony" when describing people whom he feels are not true to themselves or others. Consumers, like Holden, **can't stand a phony**. Microsoft learned this lesson all too well when a supposedly spontaneous employee dance party at its new retail outlets was exposed for what it was: an obvious fabrication designed to appear "cool."

For a while now, Apple has dominated cool when it comes to computing and consumer electronics. To better connect with consumers and combat Apple, Microsoft launched the Microsoft stores, which bear striking similarities to your local Apple store. To further the feeling of cool, employees occasionally broke into line dancing. "Caught" on camera and posted on YouTube, this employee dance number would have been fine if it were there just to generate attention and get a few laughs, that is, if the videotaping and posting were actually made by a "man on the street."

The YouTube posting was from an "average joe" who was "floored by the experience." An "anonymous poster" commented on how much "the employees must love working there." We use quotes heavily here because the posting was obviously from Microsoft or its proxy PR firms—and people immediately **picked up on the phony situation**.

Suddenly, a funny dance wasn't the story. The story became about Microsoft's fauxauthenticity and its lame sales pitch. The blogosphere (which is always up for an old-fashioned brand bashing) lit up, **ridiculing Microsoft's failed attempt at social networking**, not to mention the comments on YouTube, which were particularly brutal and not suitable to be repeated here. As Microsoft now knows, any attempt at **being anything less than genuine** and authentic about your brand, product, or service **will be exposed**.

Case Study: Arming Employees for Authenticity

Best Buy, known for the knowledgeable nerds in its Geek Squad, has a long history of encouraging employees to become experts and advocates of certain products. **Zappos**, the online shoe and clothing store, skyrocketed to success on the strength of its customer service and authentic interactions. Let's check in and see how these brands use Twitter to communicate authenticity.

@TWELPFORCE

Best Buy recently created Twelpforce, a corps of over 2,000 employees charged with helping customers via Twitter. Individual employees give customers real answers, not canned ones formulated by the PR department. While Best Buy gives this ragtag team of tech enthusiasts *some* instruction on what to say, it doesn't put words in their mouths. In many ways, employees are given free rein, which makes their interactions all the more natural.

@ZAPPOS

Checking out the **Zappos Twitter** account doesn't get you just the Zappos corporate feed. You'll also have access to the personal feeds of a few hundred Zappos employees. Each of these employees puts a face to Zappos' public identity, letting people see that this is a company with real people working at it.

WHY IT MATTERS

True authenticity only happens when the people speaking for your brand are immersed in it—and these Zappos and Best Buy employees are definitely immersed. They sell authenticity. They sell human interaction. They convey to consumers a passion for the brand that a filtered corporate message just can't deliver.

FORGET THE STAGED PHOTOS—SHOW US THE MESSY HAIR

Recent James Bond and Batman films involve a lot less camp and a lot more grit than prior films, because Hollywood has adopted a more realistic portrayal of these iconic characters. Killer box office results showed that consumers loved it. Social marketing is bringing the same level of realism to marketers.

Typical advertising embraces the cleaned-up school of thought, assembling a cast of well-groomed actors to play the all-American family, and then posing them in front of pristine beaches for a vacation shot. Looking at the photo of this happy family, you'd be pretty sure they wake up with perfectly coiffed hair and instant smiles. This family might be 100% perfect, but they're also **100% fake—and nobody can relate to that. We want the messy hair, the grit; the realism**.

TripAdvisor is a social network that rejects the glossy advertising paradigm. It takes an **authentic approach**, letting real people post real photos and videos from their trips. While the people in these pictures might at times look unkempt or exhausted, that's something we can all relate to. **It's real**. **It's authentic**. Over 25 million monthly visitors to TripAdvisor confirm the desire for authenticity.

Disney has combined the staged photo shoots with a TripAdvisor feed on its own website, allowing visitors to get honest (and unedited) assessments of real people's trips to the Magic Kingdom. Disney's gutsy move oozes authenticity. For a consumer trying to decide if he or she should take a trip to see Mickey and the gang, TripAdvisor tells it like it is.

TRANSPARENCY DOESN'T MEAN GIVING UP YOUR EDGE

The social media movement has made consumers want businesses to operate with transparency, to make everything an interactive experience. Communication might have changed, but businesses are still businesses, and they need to keep things under wraps to stay in business. Still, sharing a bit of your top-secret information with fans is **an opportunity to create intensive focus groups** that'll make fans feel special and give you the valuable data you need to stay in the black.

Burt's Bees did this with its "velvet rope" social network, in which select loyalists could access new marketing campaigns and give product feedback. Fans were thrilled by having their opinions valued, and they rewarded their favorite Earth-friendly brand by giving a heads-up on what marketing campaigns would work and which would flop.

IT'S NOT ABOUT HOW YOU FALL—IT'S ABOUT HOW YOU GET UP

In the old days, a brand did its best to appear infallible, but nowadays people don't accept that as authentic. People aren't perfect, and they are smart enough to know brands aren't, either. When a brand owns up to its mistakes, it is a chance to showcase its **humility**, its **willingness to listen**, and its **willingness to change**. These are all qualities people find refreshing and will reward.

   A few years ago, you probably heard about a **JetBlue** plane being left on the tarmac for nearly half a day, confining its passengers without food, water, or bathroom access. In response to the public outcry, JetBlue didn't cite FAA regulation or blame the ice storm that caused the incident. Instead, it admitted it had been wrong and told people what it was doing to fix it. As long as an organization hasn't been cheating consumers out of their money or putting them at risk, people are surprisingly willing to forgive a brand for its error in judgment and support its quest to correct that error.

REMEMBER, BOTH LOVERS AND HATERS GET THEIR SAY

Whatever your brand may be, it doesn't exist in a vacuum. Social media has made your brand open to adoring acclaim from **lovers** and vulnerable to vicious attacks from **haters**. If somebody has a bad experience with you, Twitter, Facebook, and email will amplify that person's voice, making his or her complaints go further. However, haters will be held accountable for their words, because **social media conversations are self-correcting**. If someone's post is blatantly misleading, you can bet there will be a horde of people ready to debunk the fallacious statement.

Just look at Wawa's many user-generated fan pages throughout the Interwebs. When someone posted a comment about how he felt Wawa breakfast sandwiches were an unhealthy, fatty way to start your day, Wawa loyalists came to its defense, comparing the nutritional facts on Wawa's egg-white sandwiches to what competitors were serving up for breakfast. These fans demonstrated that you could do a lot worse health-wise than stopping off at Wawa on your way to work. Wawa didn't even have to get its hands dirty by fighting off the attacker—it just had to stand back and let its fans manage the criticism.

BRÜNO WAS WORSE THAN A NASTY *HANGOVER*, AND SOCIAL MEDIA LET EVERYONE KNOW

There is now a public forum, unlike any other, for people to share their experiences, so your brand is accountable for all its actions. Two recent Hollywood films illustrate this point wonderfully. *Brüno* and *The Hangover* were released around the same time, to the same target audience. *Brüno* had an aggressive marketing strategy and cashed in with an amazing Friday night box office tally. But the movie stunk, and word got around. Ticket sales plummeted the next day, and the film was soon relegated to the bargain-basement theaters. *Time* magazine stated, "*Brüno* could be the first movie defeated by the Twitter effect."

The Hangover, on the other hand, didn't have as much marketing power behind it, but audiences actually liked it. It had a slow, steady growth, thanks to great word of mouth.

In this case, the studio that released *Brüno* had a great marketing department but put out a terrible product—and the studio was held accountable for that. All the marketing in the world couldn't stop the social media blitz that declared *Brüno* a dud.

chapter six

GET THAT MOTIVATION IN LINE

There's a great photography studio in Wilmington, Delaware, called LittleNest Portraits. The studio is an offshoot of the celebrity-wedding photographer and expert marketer, Laura Novak. LittleNest specializes in children's portraits, but it's also **a student of human motivation**. After LittleNest captures your beloved little one at play, you'll be emailed a link to see how the photo shoot turned out. And here's where it gets fun: if you can get ten friends to comment on the photograph on the LittleNest blog, you'll receive a free 8X10 print. Easy to implement and fun for customers, it's a **good motivator** for several other reasons.

IT GIVES PARENTS A REASON TO SPREAD THE WORD ABOUT LITTLENEST PORTRAITS.

Who doesn't want to show off their adorable kid? Most parents have a group of friends or family they've been keeping up-to-date on Junior's development via Facebook and email, so this is a natural extension.

IT BRINGS NEW CONSUMERS (THE FRIENDS OF THESE PARENTS) INTO THE MIX.

Parents of young kids tend to know other parents, so the people they send the pictures to are more likely to be more interested in children's photography than the average person on the street. These people might be impressed enough to check out LittleNest for themselves after leaving their comments on the site.

IT GETS PEOPLE INTERACTING WITH THE COMPANY.

In the social marketing world, **interaction** is the first step to a financial **transaction**.

LittleNest Portraits understands **aligned motivation**. **Whatever you ask consumers to do must support your overall brand**, like LittleNest Portraits asking people to pass along children's photos. In addition, the things your brand gives away must attract your true supporters, rather than people just interested in getting free stuff. LittleNest nails this, giving away something that's only of value to its customers.

If your business sells candlesticks, and you offer consumers a gift card to an amusement park, that motivation isn't aligned. There's no logical overlap between people who want to spend a day with Mickey and the gang and those who want to enjoy a candlelit dinner at home.

1. TRANSACTION
2. INTERACTION

Case Study: Herr's Is In Line with Fans Needs

Herr's Foods, a manufacturer of snack foods, potato chips, pretzels, and corn chips, asked us to help it start building relationships with its consumers on Facebook. Fans of Herr's had already created some unofficial fan pages on Facebook, so we wanted to generate some excitement for joining the official Herr's fan page. During the initial launch of the fan page, we asked fans to post pictures of themselves with their favorite flavor of Herr's products. Every week, Herr's would randomly select an entrant and reward him or her with a free case of potato chips. The contest was a success, adding thousands of Herr's fans and building the base for future conversations. One of the winners was a soldier stationed in Afghanistan, who sent in a great photo of his squad, each soldier with a different flavor of Herr's chips in hand!

WHY IT'S A "GOOD GIVEAWAY"

Herr's wasn't giving away a free car (which *anyone* would want). The giveaway was designed with **aligned motivation** in mind, with the prize appealing only to Herr's fans. If you weren't interested in the brand, then being rewarded with a few bags of cheddar and sour cream chips wouldn't motivate you. In addition, the **interaction** from fans—photos with their favorite flavor of chips online—was closely aligned with the brand itself and showed a vibrant community to new visitors.

MCCLELLAND'S "THEORY OF LEARNED NEEDS"

David McClelland , a psychologist who was known for his work with human motivation, theorized that different people were motivated by different things. **McClelland's "Theory of Learned Needs"** says that people are motivated by the following: a desire to achieve, a need to be affiliated with something, and a hunger for power. While people have a tendency to scoff at a psychological theory from the 1950s, McClelland's ideas have wisdom to offer to brands. First and foremost, brands **must understand what motivates people**, if they want to influence what they do as consumers.

ACHIEVEMENT

We all use goals to get ourselves off the couch and into the world. Give people a chance to achieve something (notoriety, fame, or acclaim) and they'll be motivated to engage your brand. GeoSocial Network's foursquare offers badges based upon accomplishing certain tasks, such as earning an Adventurer badge for checking in at ten different places, or a "Bender" badge for checking in four days in a row. These badges are viewable by others, visibly showing the achievements and encouraging others to earn their own.

AFFILIATION

To paraphrase your mother, you are defined by the brands you keep. Baseball fans affiliate themselves with their favorite team by donning caps and jerseys. If you cultivate coolness, consumers will be motivated to interact with you because of how that association makes them feel. Facebook users show their affiliation through their fan pages, telling the world what brands they like and want to hear from.

POWER

Who doesn't like having things their way? The chance to wield power is a strong motivator for some people, as the city of Santa Cruz discovered. When it had to cut the budget, it invited its citizens to decide how to trim the municipal fat. The local government opened itself up for suggestions, and then let the people vote for the plan they liked best. Usually a budget cut results in a public outcry, but because **people were given power** to participate in the process, the citizens were motivated to engage, rather than condemn city hall.

FIVE AREAS OF SOCIAL MARKETING MOTIVATION

McClelland's Learned Needs aren't limited to the research library. These needs serve as the foundation for understanding the motivations of social marketing. People all want to be something, and as a brand you've got to **give them the opportunity to be who they want to be**.

1. Be the Comedian

We all may not be as funny as Larry David (or even Larry the Cable Guy), but that doesn't mean a part of us doesn't want to be the one on stage making people laugh. **Create opportunities for people to be funny** via cool content, and they'll be compelled to send that message out to others. Samuel L. Jackson fans got a chance to send friends personalized phone messages promoting *Snakes on a Plane*. Choosing from a variety of funny phrases, people could personalize the message by entering their name and the name, phone number, and a few details of a friend. Soon people all over the country were getting over-the-top phone calls from Sam Jackson himself. The movie studio won by increasing the buzz about the film, and the message senders won by getting to feel like they were kings of comedy. Surprising to many, the movie about reptiles loose on a flight actually made money.

2. Be the Philanthropist

People may be motivated by *self-interest*, but that doesn't mean they're *selfish*. Altruism is a powerful motivator, as evidenced by the number of people using Facebook to show their support for the issues they care about. If your brand takes part in a cause, it's a great way to start up conversations with people who care about the same things.

As we talked about in chapter 4, that's what we did with Gore's "Warm and Fuzzy" campaign. Gore teamed up with three charities, each outdoors related, and pledged to donate money based upon how many people logged on to the "Warm and Fuzzy" website and voted for one of the charities. The charities sent out the initial messages to their supporters to make them aware of the campaign—and the fans took it from there, inviting friends to visit the "Warm and Fuzzy" site. We created a graphic visualization that represented how many people each individual had reached—showing just how contagious a little altruism can be.

3. Be the Expert

Everyone likes being recognized as an expert on something, whether it's knowing all about Edward Cullen's vampire family in *Twilight,* or being historically *savvy* enough to know which portly U.S. head of state once got stuck in a bathtub. A quiz is a great way for a brand to **tap into that desire to appear smart** and give people a chance to show off their brains.

The quiz topic should be connected to your brand but doesn't have to be *about* your brand—it just needs to be aligned with it. For instance, VH1 wouldn't get too many takers on a quiz about its channel's corporate structure, but it *would* interest pop culture fanatics with a quiz about the '80s. Give people the chance to show off their smarts, and they will. In turn, **they'll be sharing your brand** by publishing their quiz results.

4. Be the Maven

Malcolm Gladwell talks about **mavens** in his book *The Tipping Point*, those trendsetters and early adopters who just have to be on the cutting edge of a social trend. These mavens like to share with others their latest purchase or music on their iPod. If you can create a motivation with a subliminal message of "Be the first to share this with others," mavens will take the bait and spread the word.

5. Be Recognized

Norm from the sitcom *Cheers* received a warm "Norm!" from the bartender every time he walked in. This recognition is appealing to all of us and is why we return to places where "everyone knows our name."

The same is true in the social marketing world. If you show your consumers you know them, they will want to return and participate further. Frozen dessert chain **Tasti D-lite** connects the social network foursquare with its TastiRewards program. This connection enables Tasti D-lite to reward those who check in with news about specials. The one who checks in via foursquare the most, a.k.a. the mayor, receives discounts on treats. Since all the other foursquare users can see who currently holds the title, the mayor gets a tub-sized amount of recognition.

Case Study: Hit the Mark With an Exclusive Club

The producers of high end bourbon, Maker's Mark, honors a select group of fans by making them "Maker's Mark Ambassador." By doing so, it attempts to give fans an online forum for celebrating the brand, in hopes that that enthusiasm will translate into increased sales and brand recognition in the real world. Bill Samuels, Jr., Maker's Mark's president, explains the purpose: "We're not shy about telling them that as an ambassador, their job is to go out and tell other people in the world how great Maker's Mark is."

THE CLUB

The club section of the Maker's Mark website is strictly members only, but you don't have to buy a certain quota of bourbon to gain access. Anyone old enough to legally drink can sign up to be an ambassador and start enjoying special privileges. Ambassadors receive personalized business cards emblazoned with the Maker's Mark logo, as well as their name on a barrel of bourbon, which ambassadors can follow through the six-year distilling process. Maker's Mark also regularly surprises ambassadors with branded items, from holiday wrapping paper to golf balls. These items make it easy for the ambassador to show his or her affiliation with Maker's Mark, be the maven, and feel special all in one. Regular messages from company

President Bill Samuels, Jr., remind the ambassador of the affiliation and keep the bonfire stoked.

WHY IT MATTERS

For ambassadors, much of the "value" in Maker's Mark bourbon is not *in* the product at all, but in those intangibles the product provides: luxury, status, and notoriety. Don't get us wrong—Maker's Mark makes great bourbon—but there are plenty of other brands that'll come out of the bottle just as smoothly. With its online ambassadors club, Maker's Mark sells an experience—and it rewards fans in ways that reinforce that experience.

The personalized plaques and business cards are of little value for people who aren't fans of the brand, but they hold a lot of value for the loyalists who want to be special to the brand. Maker's Mark takes this desire to be special, and leverages it into making their fans their top spokespeople, which is a lot less expensive and a lot more effective than hiring a celebrity to do the job.

chapter seven

NOBODY PUTS SOCIAL IN THE CORNER

When a customer buys a faulty product, he or she doesn't get mad at a company's quality control department— the customer gets angry with the entire company. Conversely, when that company's shipping department saves the day by shipping a new product overnight, the entire company gets credit. If consumers don't distinguish between departments, then neither should your social marketing strategy.

Social marketing can't be contained in its own neat, little compartment. In fact, you might as well **nuke your Twitter department right now**—because you can't expect all social media interactions to be channeled through one point. Instead, you should weave social marketing throughout everything you do—from marketing to sales to customer service—and you can really maximize its power. Organizations need to adopt the mantra "We're all marketers now" and embrace the fact that all employees are de facto spokespeople for your brand.

WHY LEAVE YOUR BEST SHOOTERS ON THE BENCH?

In game five of the 1997 NBA Finals, the Chicago Bulls were locked in a battle with the Utah Jazz. Bulls all-star shooting guard Michael "Air" Jordan had a battle of his own, fighting a stamina-crushing flu. Air Jordan left everything on the floor and shot 38 points, giving the Bulls the win. Michael's flu-ravaged body was so drained that he had to be almost carried off the floor by teammate Scottie Pippen. Imagine if coach Phil Jackson went without Michael, deciding to keep him on the bench. The outcome of that game and the entire championship might have been very different.

You are locked in a battle with your competition every day to win the hearts, minds, and wallets of your consumers. Your employees are your "Michael Jordan";

use them! The role of the chief marketer is shifting from being the team on the court to the coach on the sideline. Your company is strong. You've got good employees, and they're just waiting to help shape your public message. It's time to put them on the court.

Get your employees on the floor. They can act as your eyes, ears, and marketing mouths, protecting and promoting your brand at a pace and authenticity that are impossible to replicate with hierarchy and press releases. In the process, your employees will see firsthand how your brand is being perceived, both good and bad, and begin to hear the voice of the customer on a regular basis.

SOCIAL ABHORS A VACUUM

With over half a billion posts, tweets, videos, and comments being posted to social sites every day, it is safe to assume that someone is talking about your brand. And if your employees aren't allowed to partake in the conversation, who will fill that void? Ex-employees? Ill-informed bloggers? To borrow a phrase from the gun lobbyists, if social is outlawed in your company, then only outlaws will have social. **You hired adults, not dolts**. Give them the tools and guidance to talk about your brand with your consumers.

KEEP THE LAWYERS AT BAY

Don't crush your employees' spirit with a 42-page corporate blogging policy. You already have rules regarding bad behavior, regardless of the medium. Employees just need to understand the reach of their conversations in the world of social. CEO of publicly traded Thomas Nelson Publishers Michael Hyatt came up with this simple guideline for his 600 employees: **"Use whatever social media you want. Feel free to use it on company time. Just use common sense and remember that if you publicly identify yourself with the company's brand then act in a manner consistent with that brand. It's in all of our best interests to do so."**

Some other suggestions when educating employees

EMPLOYEES SHOULD UNDERSTAND THE IMPACT OF THEIR ACTIONS.

Coca-Cola employees already know it's a bad idea to give away their employer's famous secret formula, but knowing to keep other, less glamorous trade secrets under wraps won't be as apparent. Make sure your employees know the difference between internal conversations and public conversations.

GUIDELINES ARE ABOUT THE POSITIVES.

While you'll have to explain what *not* to talk about, don't make the guidelines a list of things not to do. Instead, guidelines should focus on how much good for the brand employees can do through these interactions.

PREPARE THEM FOR THE WORST.

No matter who you are or how great your product is, there are people out there trash talking your brand. Teach employees to be calm and cool when confronted by detractors. Parenting experts say yelling doesn't work, and typing in ALL CAPS doesn't work in the online world, either.

EXPLAIN THE TOOLS.

Social tools offer different ways to be selective in what everyone can see. Show everyone how different privacy settings work to better control what the public might see.

MAKE PARTICIPATION OPTIONAL.

Not everyone has to tweet or open up their Facebook account to customers. These types of interactions aren't for everyone. But those employees who do choose to engage the customer will have an invaluable consumer perspective. The savvy employees will understand this and will want to join the conversations.

DITCH "FIRE, FORGET, AND MEASURE"—IT'S TIME TO EMBRACE "LAUNCH, LISTEN, AND IMPROVE"

With traditional marketing, you've got to be a forecaster of sorts—but instead of predicting next week's weather, you're trying to divine what consumers will respond to four or five months down the road. In a traditional campaign, you put most of the work in up front, getting the campaign ready and selecting spots that will reach the right demographic. After that, you **fire it off** to the publishers and essentially **forget about it** until it's released a few months later. When the ad comes out, you look at the reports to try to **measure how effective the campaign was**. What were the reach and frequency on that effort? Did it move the needle? And *after that*? Usually, there is no after that. The campaign is finished, and you go on to the next one.

In contrast, if you integrate social marketing aspects into your traditional marketing campaign, you can improve upon this process. Social marketing's **launch**, **listen**, and **improve** strategy lets you get immediate feedback and modify your campaign as it's happening. The moment you **launch a campaign**, use social media to listen to **people's initial reactions**. Is Twitter alight with re-tweets and praise, or do the comments on your Facebook wall read like a grand jury indictment? This feedback will inform how to move forward with your campaign, implementing the changes necessary to make your ads more effective. If people love or hate aspects of what you're doing, shift your message to emphasize the popular parts, and ditch the parts that people hate.

Effective marketing campaigns need to be fluid. From the outset, you've got to give yourself leeway to change your message. That way, you can **improve the campaign** based on what you learn by listening to the digital masses.

Case Study: Financial Crisis Leads to Better Listening Skills

Vail Resorts is one of North America's largest ski resort companies, with five resorts and over a billion dollars in annual revenue. Historically, the company spent most of its advertising budget in the top travel and outdoor magazines, which typically required ads to be submitted four to five months prior to publication. When the financial crisis hit in 2008, Vail Resorts had already spent their advertising dollars in print and were left with a smaller pot with which to market in a vastly changed economy and consumer buying habits. According to Vail Resorts' CEO, Rob Katz, last-minute vacations were becoming the norm. The highly coveted week between Christmas and New Year's, which is normally booked in June, went from 50% occupancy to over 80% in the week before Christmas. Vail Resorts needed new flexibility to compete.

RESPONSE TO THE CRISIS.

Vowing not to make the same mistake the next year, Vail Resorts pulled most of its print ad budget for use in more flexible advertising formats, such as newspaper, radio, and web. More importantly, they used social networks to **listen to what worked** and what didn't work. They were able to couple this with real-time booking data to try

(continued)

(continued)

new promotions, listen to the response, and then adjust accordingly. Vail Resorts was able to keep pace with consumers and fine-tune a highly flexible campaign.

WHY IT MATTERS

John Wanamaker famously said, "I know that half of my advertising dollars are wasted...I just don't know which half." By listening to what was working, Vail Resorts was able to shift their message based upon what was working. Now you can hear millions of voices in a way that hasn't been possible before. You can hear immediately whether a campaign is hitting or not and react accordingly.

GIVING SOCIAL A LITTLE LOVE

You understand that hearing the voice of the consumer is important, and you want the rest of your team to come on board and be able to hear it, too. But how do you sell social marketing to your team?

Put social on your meeting agenda.

Lead by example, and show everyone how much you value social marketing by bringing it up at meetings. Talk about its applications and about weaving it throughout your business. You've got to raise your team's awareness before the team hops on board.

Don't leave it up to the interns.

They're young and they look tech-savvy, but that doesn't mean you should hand them the keys to your Twitter and Facebook accounts. Doing so says that you don't really think social marketing is that important. Consider Pizza Hut, which put out ads trying to find social media interns (Twinterns) to "manage Pizza Hut's social media presence." According to the article in *The New York Times*, "the successful applicant will speak fluent OMG and LOL and correctly use the terms DM (direct message), RT (retweet) and # (hashtag)." That tells us that Pizza Hut doesn't really understand social, that it just wants to give it some face time. If you want to effect real change in the way you do business, putting the person with the least pull in your organization in charge of your social marketing effort isn't the way to go.

Put your star players in the game.

Assigning your top talent to handle social marketing sends the message that you're serious about it. Your star players have the talent to weave social media throughout your company, and because they're the best at what they do, people in power are more likely to give them free rein. With these innovative people doing their thing, every marketing campaign should be able to answer the question, "How are we going to engage the consumer using social media?" That's how you start to weave social marketing into the rest of your efforts.

Ask yourself how often you listen.

Consumers are always talking. How often are you listening? We aren't talking about occasionally googling your company to see what pops up. This kind of intermittent listening is more for fun than for real research purposes. No, we mean *really* listen. Listen to what you're doing right, and put even more energy in those areas. Listen to the complaints to see what you can do better. Decide that the voice of the consumer is the voice you're going to use to influence the future of your marketing direction. Social media lets you hear the consumer's voice without having to shell out money to buy coffee and donuts for a focus group.

REASSURE MANAGEMENT THAT YOU HAVE SOCIAL UNDER CONTROL

Once you have the team on board, you next need to get the rest of the management team on board. This may be the most challenging part!

DEMYSTIFY

Getting managers to shed their long-held belief of command and control is no small task, since many probably have never seen a Facebook/Twitter. Make sure everyone has seen social in action and knows the lingo.

OVERWHELM

A couple of searches will showcase thousands of conversations happening around your brand. Make sure the team sees the sheer number of conversations going on right now that require attention. Go ahead and show the team what the competition is doing with social, just to let everyone feel a sense of urgency.

DEMYSTIFY

OVERWHELM

COMMIT

REPORT

COMMIT

Even the most supportive team will have reservations. Reassure the managers that you have the proper oversight for listening to the conversations and a sound "crisis management" plan that can be activated quickly.

REPORT

At every meeting, present your "social dashboard," with key stats, snippets of conversations, successes, and learnings. This real-time data will become addicting for management, so make sure that you have a plan to easily produce this data on a regular basis.

chapter eight

ASSEMBLING YOUR A-TEAM

In 1943, Lockheed Aircraft was faced with a challenge: it needed to come up with a new aircraft frame to support jets, and it needed to do it quickly. By 1943, WWII was in full force, the Germans were ahead of the game, and the U.S. government was putting on the pressure. A young engineer for Lockheed by the name of Clarence L. "Kelly" Johnson had a plan for how to structure this airframe and presented it to the U.S. Air Force. Two days later, the government said, "Build it," and Lockheed "Skunk Works" was born.

143 days later, the first American jet airplane was delivered, arguably altering American history for the foreseeable future.

In order to deliver something that had never been conceived of, under a strict timeline and the pressure of winning a war, Kelly had to think differently and make sure that the solution he built could be spread throughout the bureaucratically burdened organization. Kelly had to break all the rules that once stifled innovation and creativity. Before even getting started, Kelly laid out his 14 rules of operation. In summary, the most pertinent rules revolved around getting a small and relevant team on board, keeping things simple and direct, incorporating measurable results, and giving the right access to the right information while regarding the results of the task—not the number of people being managed (which had commonly become the case in the early 20th century).

Moving your marketing online into the social medium will require your own "Skunk Works" mentality, and as the CMO, you're the new Kelly Johnson. Fear not—the upside is tremendous, just as it was for Lockheed and our country in the 1940s. Understand that what is at stake is very measurable and can affect the way those outside and inside your walls interact with your brand. You'll need to assemble the right team and draw out your plan with the right rules, which are unique to your organization.

ASSEMBLE YOUR A-TEAM

The 1980s TV series "The A-Team" put a ragtag collection of ex-special forces characters together to solve mysteries and fight crime. Each week, the show's writers drew upon the individual talents of the co-stars to get out of a tough situation and save the day. Hannibal made the plans, The Face smooth-talked his way through tough situations, Murdock flew the plane over the cuckoo's nest, and B.A. had the muscles and the mechanical skills to keep the team running. To successfully implement social marketing throughout your business, you need to assemble your own A-Team.

Your A-Team will consist of the best people from various departments in your organization. And it's no place for interns—after all, **would you hand the task of creating a branding strategy to an intern**? You need people who are more than just familiar with your brand; you need people who live and breathe the brand.

By assembling your A-Team, you are **defining the role the rest of your organization is going to play** and getting the right people on board to make things happen. If you're a small company, it could be just five people, but a large company's A-Team might include 30 dedicated employees. Here's whom you'll need:

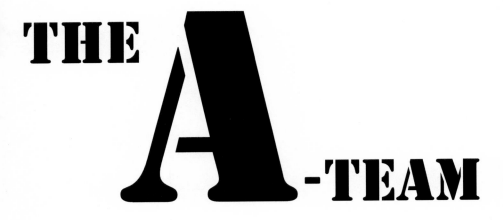

THE DIGITAL GENIUS.

This person needs to understand and embrace the constantly evolving platforms. If this person were a part of a team on a television show, he or she would be the glasses-wearing geek with a knack for gadgets and computer hacking. But today's digital geniuses are proving there's nothing uncool about having a passion for being in the digital marketplace. It isn't enough to put a traditional designer on your team, no matter how talented he or she is. You need someone with a proven track record of utilizing different forms of social media effectively.

THE CONTENT CREATORS.

These folks don't find the confines of a 30-second radio spot prohibitive, because they're used to getting their point across within the 140-*character* limit of a tweet. Your content creators will understand what comes across well in a social marketing campaign, and what should be left to traditional marketing. Your content creators should understand your brand and the message you're trying to convey, because one poorly-thought-out tweet or one toxic blog post can bring down your whole social campaign.

THE LISTENER.

This A-Teamer is like a digital doctor, able to tell whether your campaign has a strong pulse or if it's flatlining. By reading the online responses to your campaign, he or she analyzes how you're doing and informs you how to best move forward. He or she will also keep you apprised of what the competition is up to and make sure your company knows about new developments in the social media world.

KEY PEOPLE FROM OTHER DEPARTMENTS.

Effective social marketing isn't confined to one department; it's weaved throughout an organization. Grab someone from the e-Commerce, Regulatory, Fulfillment, and Sales departments. These people will add a base of knowledge to your team that is hard to find within a marketing department.

IT'S ALL PART OF THE PLAN

Now that you've assembled your A-Team, how do you get the rest of your organization on your side? For one, you've got to address their concerns that you want to radically change their work lives and your organization's image.

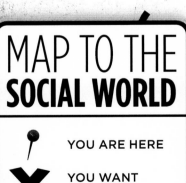

MAP TO THE
SOCIAL WORLD

 YOU ARE HERE

✗ YOU WANT
TO BE HERE

ROAD TO THE
SOCIAL WORLD

Before you can get down to the gritty details of how you're going to take the social world by storm, you need a broad plan outlining your goals. Define where you are going and what you are trying to accomplish. Develop a social strategic plan first and the tactics for implementing it later. But don't worry if you don't feel like you have a contingency plan for every situation. There are a lot of things that might come up once you enter the social arena, and it's OK not to know how you'll handle all of them. Prepare for the situations you can anticipate, but plan to make mistakes, because everyone does.

LEARN FROM THE SUCCESSES (AND FAILURES) OF OTHERS

Get your own healthy dose of listening to those who have ventured into social before you. Reach out to your peers in these organizations. Don't just pay attention to companies similar to yours—look at all sorts of efforts by various companies.

One thing that often discourages the decision makers in an organization is how much social marketing actually costs. The misconception is that social marketing is cheap. The resources you use (Facebook, Twitter, etc.) are free, but coming up with a great plan and implementing it successfully are not. It's not like slapping up a billboard: you can't appear to be giving a sales pitch. Instead, you've got to engage customers, and doing this effectively takes time and money. Show the people in your organization examples of successes other companies have had, and they'll be more likely to sign off on a social marketing program.

LOOK AT YOUR BRAND BEFORE MAKING YOUR GRAND ENTRANCE.

Everything your brand has done so far will affect how you enter the social world. Are you an established organization or are you just getting off the ground? Established brands have already been putting out messages for years, and consumers have preconceived notions about who they are and what they do. These organizations have a bigger ship to turn, so to speak, while new organizations have a fresh slate.

In addition, you should honestly assess how consumers feel about your brand. If you've got a strong connection with consumers (like Wawa or Herr's), interactions celebrating the brand work well. For the insurance company whose customers feel little personal connection to it, campaigns focusing on product building or customer service play out better.

DETERMINE YOUR PURPOSE

What do you hope to gain by entering the social arena? Whether it's improved customer service, insight into product development, or a better understanding of the consumer, you need to know why you're entering the social world before you do. First and foremost, whatever your purpose is, you need to make sure that the principles of your organization are not violated in your upcoming campaign. Once you know your purpose, you can determine what media will work best for your needs. Will Twitter, Facebook, or blog entries suit your purposes best?

Case Study: What You Can Learn From ING Direct

When ING Direct interacts in the social world, it doesn't do it haphazardly. It uses its most talented people and implement a plan after tossing around ideas and thinking about their implications. However, this doesn't mean ING Direct's social media interactions are held back by a lot of red tape. Instead, ING Direct's top talent is trusted to interact with the public in real time.

THE CONTEST

ING Direct held a contest via Twitter in which the first ten people who correctly tweeted the number of ING Direct

(continued)

(continued)

ATMs that were within a ten-mile radius would win iPhones. Thousands of people did a quick ATM lookup and tweeted the answer for all to see. The promotion was a success and raised awareness that ING Direct had a high ATM density.

While most promotions take six months to plan and implement, this one was carried out in one afternoon. How was this quick promotion possible? The real story behind it lies in the creation of a special team dedicated to engaging the public with social media.

DEVELOPMENT OF THE TEAM

The idea for a social marketing team originated in the marketing department, where a few members had been meeting every day to discuss what they'd been learning about the burgeoning social marketplace. Initially, they met for two hours a day, but soon they moved some tables together in the center of the department and bounced ideas off one another for half the day.

The more they talked, the more they realized others outside the marketing department needed to be brought in. So these enterprising marketers went to management and said they wanted to concentrate on social marketing

(continued)

(continued)

full time. Not only that, they brought a list of key people from other departments and said they'd like them to join the social marketing team, too. Management said yes, and what started in the marketing department now included people from all over the organization.

THE EARLY INTERACTIONS

ING Direct started with a controlled interaction: a blog. The blog could be proofread and carefully crafted, so it wasn't really risking any social media gaffes. Soon after, they took the next step and opened the blog up to public comments. Then the big moment came: ING Direct broadcasted their first tweet, which was something like "ING Direct is now entering the social world." Within five hours, they had over 300 followers.

The tweets started rolling in—a lot of good ones, and a few bad. ING Direct handled the complaints in a natural way, rather than with a pre-planned script. If a customer complained that the website was slow, the team forwarded the complaint to IT. If a customer was angry about his or her account, they forwarded the complaint to customer service.

THE REFINED INTERACTIONS

ING Direct streamlined their responses, deciding to fast-track approval of customer requests. If someone received a customer request, he or she would literally yell to whoever in the room had the authority to authorize what the customer wanted. Then that person would either grant the request or deny it. The key for ING Direct was handling complaints quickly, and it did that very well.

WHY IT MATTERS

ING Direct's social marketing effort started with a few people tossing around ideas and evolved through careful planning and bringing in the right people. Even if your organization doesn't resemble ING Direct, you can still learn from the model it developed.

chapter nine

RETHINKING ROI

As of January 2010, Herr's has 322,000 Facebook fans. It's a big number, but what does it really mean for ROI? To understand the significance of its massive fan community, remembering your high school physics class and what you learned about **potential energy** will come in handy.

Imagine there's a one-ton rock sitting on the ground. As it is, it's just a one-ton rock, nothing more. But now imagine this same rock is suspended from a steel cable, 30 stories in the air. Now this rock is *more* than just a rock; it has the potential energy to fall and have a **massive impact** on the landscape below. But this doesn't mean it *will* fall and change the ground beneath it. Even with all that potential, our one-ton rock needs someone to come along and cut the steel cable holding it. Otherwise, it'll stay where it is, inert.

Like the one-ton rock, a Facebook page without fans is just a Facebook page. Add 322,000 fans to that page, and now it has the *potential* to reach millions. But again, without a catalyst, without someone willing to cut the cord, this Facebook page will remain inert. Someone has to come along and create an engaging environment for fans to interact and **unleash the potential energy** of this Facebook page.

Let's once again look at the Facebook page for Herr's and its fans. Each "fan" has an average of over 100 friends; we can conservatively estimate that 80 of those are unique to that fan. One post then has the possibility of rippling through 25,600,000 people or free impressions. Now that's some serious potential. But how do you calculate ROI on this Facebook page?

There's a lot of talk about how you can't measure ROI on social marketing. And it's true, there are certain things you can't know. But there's also plenty you can figure out. Say Herr's rolls out a new potato chip Facebook application. We can see 127 people liked it and commented on it. We don't know how many people then rushed out to the grocery store and stocked up on Herr's, but we do know that Herr's engaged 322,000 people with an opportunity to engage more. And Herr's has done it in a higher-quality, more personal way than with a magazine ad or radio spot.

Rather than concentrating on how certain metrics from traditional marketing don't work with social, you should instead rethink ROI from the ground up when deciding how much to invest in a social marketing campaign. **Take into consideration the qualitative and quantitative benefits** and the **impact to other areas of the organization**. If you do this, you'll see that ROI for social marketing isn't just a theoretical exercise, like trying to develop cold fusion. There are real across-the-board benefits to be found.

DEFINE SUCCESS UP FRONT

There are a lot of reasons why an organization might run a social marketing campaign. You may hope to improve brand awareness, integrate social media into your customer service experience, address customer service concerns better, or simply increase sales. With each of these approaches, there will be a different return on investment that you'll want to measure.

There is not a one-size-fits-all way to measure your success. You need to **define your own goals and understand what success means for you**, because it isn't just a dollars and cents measurement. Success must include qualitative measures such as the quality of consumer engagement and quantitative measures like the number of conversations about your brand.

METRICS FOR SOCIAL MARKETING: IT'S NOT JUST ABOUT QUANTITY

It's not about having "X" number of fans. It's about having fans who are talking about you in a positive way. Here are some social marketing metrics that you can use to **define success**, and the caveats that go along with them.

THE BUZZ

How much **time do people spend discussing** your product? Is your brand getting mentioned in newspapers and popping up in Twitter feeds? These are all evidence that your marketing strategy is working. In the old days, it was all about how much time people spend listening to you, because traditional marketing was all about getting people to shut up and listen. Social marketing, on the other hand, is all about **getting people to** open up and talk about the brand.

QUALITY

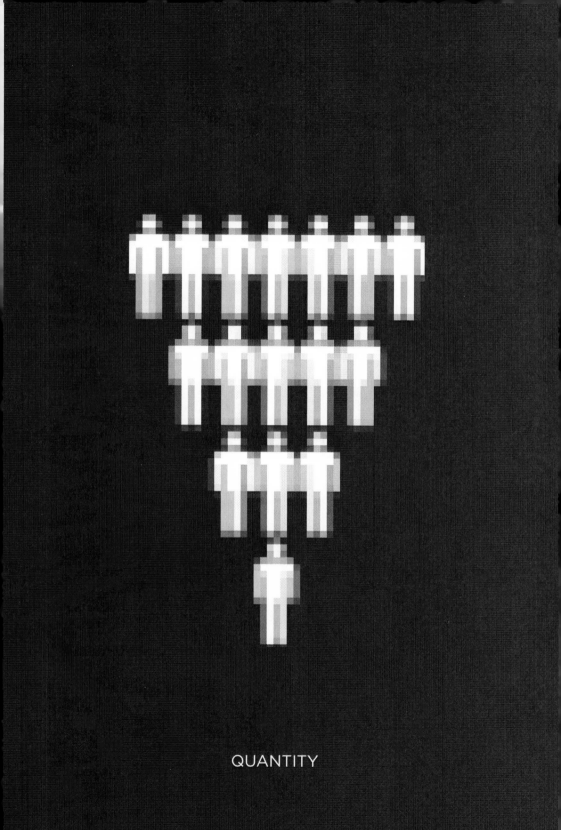

QUANTITY

THE NUMBER OF FANS

Increasing your fan base is a great goal, as long as it's just a starting point. Having 10,000 fans doesn't mean anything unless you interact with them in a meaningful way. Instead of making a goal of getting 10,000 new fans, set the dual goals of gaining new fans *and* interacting with them better. If you unleash the potential energy of your fans, you'll have thousands of people advocating for your brand.

In addition, your number of **fans can be a valuable indicator of how your social marketing is driving other aspects** of your company. When we coordinated a Comcast campaign in which people signed up for a chance to win tickets to a New Year's Day hockey game in Boston, we measured how many people entered the contest through Facebook and through tweets, and compared that number to the total number of entries. That way, we could calculate the impact social media had on the size of the contest pool.

First and foremost, we wanted people to sign up for this contest. By being able to see how many signed up as a result of social media, we were able to **assess the success of our social marketing effort**.

E-MOTIONS

People express themselves online in more subtle ways than just smiley faces and typing in all caps. When they pass on messages about you, look at what emotions are going into those messages. How do they feel about your brand? Are people happy about your product, or are they angry with your slow customer service responses? Whatever these emotions are, gauge them before and during a social marketing campaign to see what effect it's having on your audience's feelings toward your brand.

The Intangibles: A Few Things to Think About

YOU CAN'T CALCULATE ROI ON EVERYTHING.

But just because these intangibles won't show up on your end-of-the-year report doesn't mean that you shouldn't consider them when deciding how much to invest in your social marketing efforts.

IT'S NOT JUST ABOUT WHAT YOU HEAR, BUT WHOM YOU HEAR IT FROM.

Hearing something from a friend is more valuable than hearing it from an advertisement. If you're about to have a baby and are shopping around for doctors, having a friend tell you that his or her pediatrician has the magic touch with kids will mean more to you than seeing that message on TV. Maybe the television ad would reach more people, but the personal recommendation from a friend carries more weight. These conversations are now happening online through Facebook and Twitter, and smart social marketing will result in people personally recommending your brand to their friends.

YOU DON'T HAVE TO SHOOT IN THE DARK. SPEND YOUR MONEY IN AREAS THAT WORK.

Politicians are always talking about accountability when it comes to government spending. If you want *real* accountability, just look at what the social world has to offer. It might be hard to quantify ROI for social marketing, but that doesn't mean you'll be spending money blindly.

Old-school logic tells you that spending $300,000 to run an ad in *GQ* is a safe bet, but spending $50,000 on a Facebook page is risky. Look again. How often do people read back issues of *GQ*? Yes, your $300,000 ad will reach millions of people, but it has a finite lifespan and has no guarantee that it reached the right million people. There's no guarantee that those million people even *read* your ad.

A properly nurtured Facebook page, on the other hand, will continue to grow and attract new visitors, visitors who choose to engage in your conversation. Rather than running a one-time ad, you can invest money in building an ongoing relationship that won't be thrown out with last month's *GQ*. **It takes time to build the social marketing bonfire**, but once you do, it will show returns. Educate the key decision makers in your organization about this fact to encourage them to buy into social marketing.

YOU NEED SMART PEOPLE AND SMART PROGRAMS TO READ ALL THIS DATA.

In the film *The Matrix*, the simulated reality in which most of humanity lived was represented in the "real world" as green bits of data streaming on computer monitors. Neo, Morpheus, and their buddies relied on "operators," the people who could read this data from the matrix and tell them what was going on inside.

While *The Matrix* might just be science fiction, organizations really do need people who can make sense out of mountains of data. From the Google Analytics reports to the gigs' worth of log files, it's this data that will help determine ROI from social marketing. All of this data is worthless without the right tools and right people to tell you what it means.

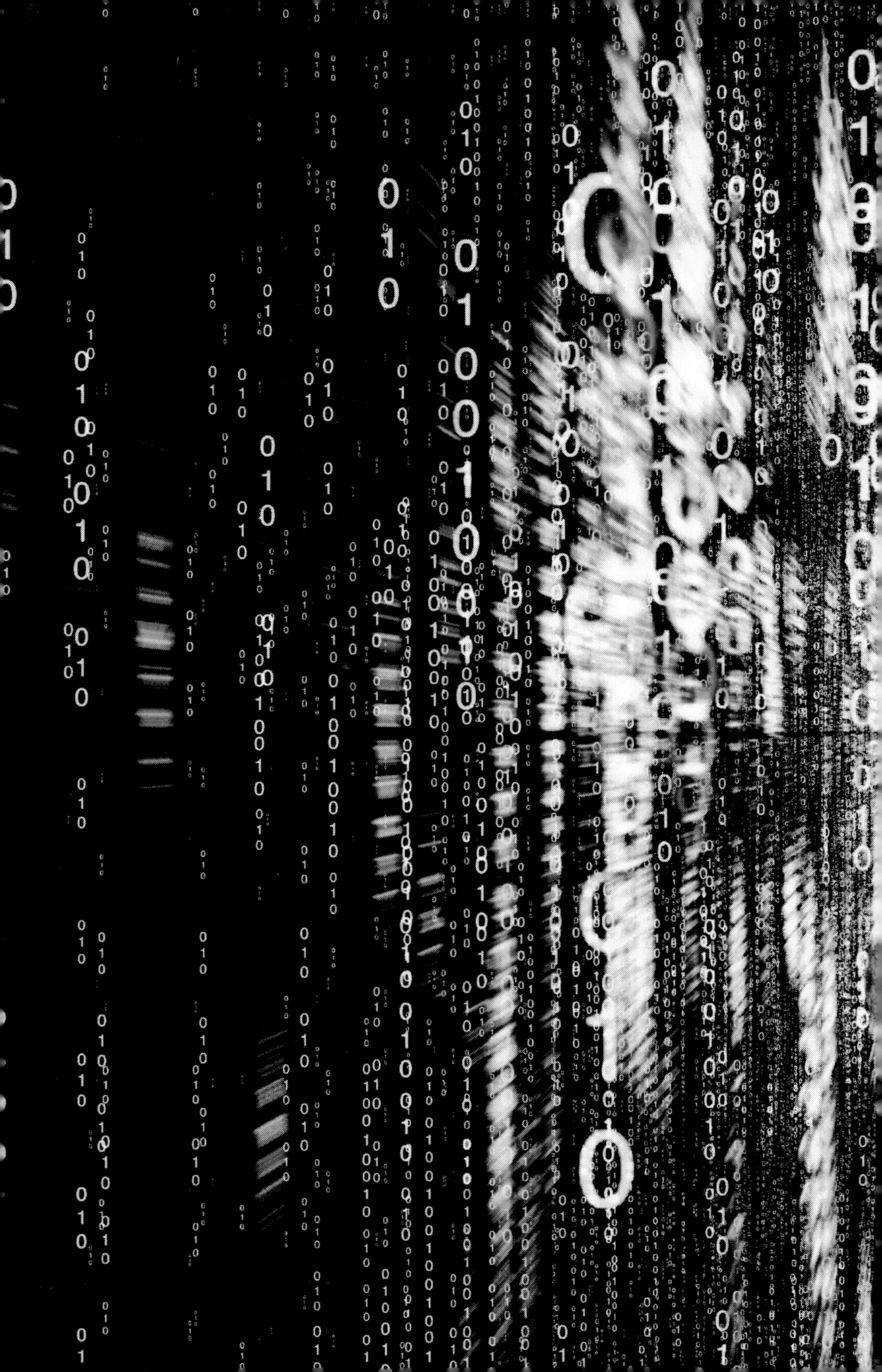

As recently as 2008, there were few programs on the market that could get a reading on ROI for social marketing efforts. But now there are automated tools that allow you to listen in on thousands of conversations at once and determine if an online interaction was good or bad for the brand. Even better, the more sophisticated programs cater their analysis to different types of businesses. For instance, a program used by a computer retailer will look for different positives and negatives than one used by a fast food restaurant trying to sell more hamburgers.

While these programs are great for going through a mass of data, they can't replace an intelligent person's keen analytical abilities. When you've got conflicting data, you're going to need a smart person there to figure out what's going on. For example, maybe the data says your sales are up, but you're also getting reports that people are expressing more negative emotions about you. Why is this happening? You need people who will be able to understand those trends and make sense of them.

CALCULATE ROI ACROSS MULTIPLE DEPARTMENTS

As we've tried to drive home for most of this book, social marketing doesn't just affect marketing; it has to do with your entire organization. For this reason, **ROI needs to be measured across multiple**

departments—and from some departments you wouldn't normally consider.

With social marketing, your organization's departments no longer exist in a void. In the past, if a bank put up a billboard, it would only affect the marketing department. But now, when social marketing launches a campaign to get new accounts, customer service will need to be brought in.

Likewise, ROI from other departments should include benefits to marketing, where appropriate. For example, say Comcast's customer service department receives a complaint via Twitter and solves that problem within five minutes. When the grateful customer tweets a thanks in response, suddenly that customer service "call" has entered the public arena (because other people can see this interaction). What historically would have been considered a customer service interaction now has had a positive impact on marketing—something that would have never occurred in the magazine ad you may have just spent $300,000 or more on.

chapter ten

WHAT'S NEXT

As I write this, Steve Jobs is on stage introducing Apple's iPad, the tablet computer that he claims will revolutionize how we use computers. Will it? Will a computer on every couch cause us to rethink social networking, just as the iPhone's app platform caused us to rethink how we use phones? The answers are unknown, and that fear of the unknown always frustrates marketers. Marketers are deathly afraid of having their annual budgets allocated in January after a "hot new concept" goes mainstream in September. Or worse, a platform goes out of favor just as a funded effort launches.

Flickr Photo by Brian Truono, www.flickr.com/trueth

Some Key Things to Watch Out For

THE "TRAGEDY OF THE COMMONS" MAY REAR ITS UGLY HEAD

Garrett Hardin coined the phrase "Tragedy of the Commons" to describe how common property can be overused and cease to be useful to everyone. This is already starting to happen on Twitter, where following a few hundred people results in an overwhelming raw feed. As platforms go mainstream, their goals go from trying increase the input of content to trying to manage the overwhelming output of content on users.

The trend is to automate our content publishing, as foursquare does by posting location updates to Facebook or Twitter. Too many tweets and nobody wants to read them. This trend in micro-sharing needs to be balanced with strong filtering to help us keep what we value front and center, or we will move to the next platform. Marketers need to be careful not to destroy their own goodwill by providing more posts but less content of value.

THE RISE OF "VELVET ROPE" SOCIAL NETWORKS

In 2009, we were conducting eyetracking studies with the University of Delaware, hoping to understand how users of Facebook review pages on the site so marketers can better reach consumers on the site. During our interview with the test subjects, we encountered a few participants who had given up their Facebook accounts because they were tired of sharing with everyone.

As a marketer, it is critical that you stay on the watch for your target audience migrating to "velvet rope" social networks, or networks that limit access based upon certain criteria. Facebook, as an example, started by only allowing those with .edu email addresses to gain access. These networks already exist today (Sermo. com, for example, is only for physicians), and as people experience the power of social networks on the major public sites, they might turn their attention to more focused conversations in these closed networks.

PRIVACY AND SOCIAL WILL CONTINUE TO FIGHT

The rise of Al Gore's World Wide Web was met with big privacy fears, fanned by the mainstream media. The social generation has set aside many of those fears, instead seeing the value exchanged for sharing more and more private information. But how far will this go? A new social service, Blippy, offers to link to your purchases or even your checking account, sharing your purchases with your friends. Will this be too personal for this social generation? Time will tell.

Marketers looking for increased focus in their marketing will want to use this data to allow further message targeting. Consumer rights advocacy organizations, largely staffed by people at least a generation behind the adopters of these new technologies, will ask the government to get involved and make sure consumers are protected. This battle between sharing and privacy will continue, and as a marketer, you have to be careful not to be held up as the poster child for bad marketing behavior.

What are you to do?

Focus on the Fundamentals

While the pace of change seems dizzying, the fundamentals remain largely constant. People are searching out meaningful conversations online; brands can participate if they play by the rules, and your organization needs to be ready to interact with people in a genuine and authentic manner. This applies as much to Twitter and Facebook as it does to foursquare, Gowalla and whatever may be next.

Stay in the Loop

Add popular social news sites such as Mashable.com or BoingBoing.net to your Twitter feed. They are reporting on the rapidly changing social media landscape, and they often report with a slightly critical eye. Keep these and other news sites on your radar.

Social Requires Masses—Ask Around

There are over 500 social networking sites, but you would be hard pressed to name more than a dozen. As you are pitched about being a part of the "next big thing," ask others to see if they have heard of this new social concept. Your customers can provide you with great feedback on what new social platforms they are interested in being a part of.

Explore Personally Before Corporately

Before you commit the company to a platform, have your team give it a test ride. This firsthand experience will not only validate the platform's hype; your team will see what other networks have to offer, how they want users to interact, etc. These learnings will keep the team current on social trends.

Failings Are Learnings—Publicize the Learnings

Oscar Wilde wrote, "Experience is simply the name we give our mistakes." There will be mistakes as you refine the right way to interact with your consumers. Avoid the first reaction, to hide these mistakes, and instead publicize or even celebrate them. Your team won't always be faced with the same question next time, but by sharing the experiences, you help your team provide the right answer to that yet-asked question.

Social Isn't a Platform; It's a Conversation

You shouldn't have a Facebook effort, a Twitter effort, etc. You need to have a social effort, focused on building conversations with consumers, wherever they might be this quarter. Approaching it as a conversation and not just a platform will keep you nimble as new trends emerge.

Jump on In!

Companies large and small are finding ways to embrace social marketing and generate positive results for their bottom line. Let us know how it is going with your social efforts. We will be highlighting great examples as we uncover them and sharing them with you on our blog:

www.EngageBlog.com.

Join the conversation!

Index

About the Authors

LEE MIKLES

As co-founder and CEO of The Archer Group, Lee provides the company's vision and overall strategy. He holds both electrical engineering and MBA degrees from the University of Delaware, making digital marketing almost the only logical career choice for Lee. Lee's digital marketing perspectives have been featured in national media outlets, including *Advertising Age* and *The Wall Street Journal*. Lee has also served as an adjunct professor at the University of Delaware, teaching Internet marketing at the Alfred Lerner School of Business.

Follow Lee on twitter.com/LMikles.

PATRICK CALLAHAN

Patrick is Archer's co-founder and COO. He focuses on harnessing innovation into repeatable processes, a skill he learned setting up Accenture's legendary Infocosm section in Philadelphia, the group Accenture formed to make sense of the powerful change agent then known as the "World Wide Web." Patrick is a graduate of Drexel University with a business and economics degree. In addition, he holds a juris doctorate from Widener University School of Law.

Patrick and Lee met during the heady dot-com days in 1999 at a Fast Company—"Company of Friends" event and immediately connected. This event was organized by professionals interested in a change of doing business "as usual." Years later, Patrick and Lee created The Archer Group with that same vision of change.

Follow Patrick on twitter.com/BigGreenBox.